P9-CFS-421

The
Gloucester Guide
A Stroll through Place and Time

The
Gloucester Guide

A Stroll through Place and Time

Joseph E. Garland

PROTEAN PRESS
Rockport, Massachusetts

To
Alison Reid Bryan

Copyright © 1990 by Protean Press and Joseph E. Garland. All rights reserved. No part of this work may be reproduced or transmitted in any form or by any means electronic or mechanical, including photocopying and recording, or by any information storage or retrieval system without permission in writing from the publisher and author.

Illustration Credits

Cape Ann Historical Association 5, 9, 11, 19, 39, 41, 42, 43, 47, 63, (by Martha Rogers Harvey) 6, 15, 58; Annisquam Historical Society 12; Magnolia Library Center (by Procter Brothers) 2; *Frank Leslie's Illustrated Newspaper* (March 27, 1875) 35; *Gloucester Master Mariners Yearbook* (1917) 57; James B. Benham collection 17, 27; Reginald H. Currier collection 7; Paul Harling collection 25; Steve Howard collection (by Procter Brothers) 3, 8, 13, 14, 36, 37, 62; William D. Hoyt collection 20; William Sawyer collection 21; Gordon W. Thomas collection 4, 24, 48, 49, 54, (by Ernest L. Blatchford) 33, 52, 53; Author's collection 1, 10, 16, 18, 22, 23, 31, 34, 40, 44, 45, 46, 55, 56, 61, (by Martha Rogers Harvey) 60, (by Adolph Kupsinel) 38, 59, (by Eben Parsons) 26, 28, 29, 30, 32, 50, 51.

Protean Press is an imprint of Editorial Inc. This title was produced cooperatively by: David Alpher (proofreader); Herb Batten (bookkeeper); David Eales (sales representative); Laura Fillmore (publisher); Joseph E. Garland (author); Jay Howland (editor); Barbara Kassabian (typesetter); David McAveeney (printer and binder); and Inga Soderberg (designer).

Printed by The Pressroom Printers, Gloucester, Massachusetts

Cover Illustration: *Gloucester Harbor* by Fitz Hugh Lane (1847). Cape Ann Historical Association.

ISBN 0-9625780-0-2

Protean Press
P.O. Box 44
Rockport, Massachusetts 01966

CONTENTS

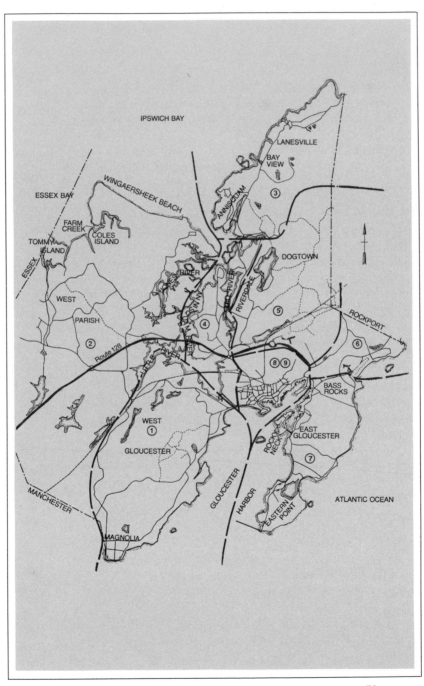

IPSWICH BAY

LANESVILLE

BAY
VIEW

ESSEX BAY

WINGAERSHEEK BEACH

FARM
CREEK

COLES
ISLAND

③

ANNISQUAM

TOMMY
ISLAND

DOGTOWN

ESSEX

RIVER

ANNISQUAM RIVER

RIVERDALE

WEST

PARISH

⑤

ROCKPORT

②

④

Route 128

⑥

LITTLE RIVER

⑧ ⑨

BASS
ROCKS

WEST

①

EAST
GLOUCESTER

GLOUCESTER

ROCKY
NECK

⑦

MANCHESTER

GLOUCESTER

HARBOR

EASTERN
POINT

ATLANTIC OCEAN

MAGNOLIA

Gloucester

PREFACE

Although seventeen years have hustled by since *The Gloucester Guide: A Retrospective Ramble* undertook to mosey through our first three hundred and fifty as the founding settlement of the Massachusetts Bay Colony, the offhandedness with which the first edition directed the reader halfway down the next block on the right persists.

"This is not really a *guide* to Gloucester at all," it warned anyone expecting anything more than a do-it-yourself handbook. "No one is guided through our myriad city, only beguiled by it. Gloucester is here, and if you would partake of it, you will do so on *its* terms, not via the megaphone of any tour director."

Quite so today, even as we enter the final decade of a century of ever-accelerating change. Gloucester's lack of self-consciousness about its uniqueness as the most diverse and second most spread-out city in the Commonwealth, and once the saltiest fishing port in the world, remains the most unique of its uniquely unique qualities.

What the heck is Joan of Arc up to, out here in Fishtown, charging the local Legionnaires behind their World War I machine guns and their out-of-place-and-time Greek Revival fortress with its peeling paint, while presenting her armored back and her horse's rump to the onslaughts of Washington Street traffic?

The question remains, although rather inadequately answered in that first, slim, pumpkin-colored edition of the *Guide*, which has been out of print for several years. So it occurred to me to find out more about our Maid of Orleans and to expand on the answers to other questions too, and to salt the dish with a few more yarns, on the assumption that if Gloucester's endless nooks and crannies continued to pique my curiosity they would yours, oh peripatetic reader, for that is what you must be, either afoot or in your armchair, to gain any benefit or pleasure whatever from what follows.

The result of these musings is this somewhat revised, moderately enlarged, and thoroughly updated second edition of *The Gloucester Guide*.

The type is larger, and there is more of it, and there are more vintage photographs, and an expanded format that still slips into a coat pocket, handbag, backpack, or glove compartment. Retracing my steps of 1972, I've incorporated most of the remarkably few changes in the face of Gloucester, which says something about our relative success—so far—in resisting the assaults on our treasured environment.

A few corners around town and a cache of stories that didn't make the first edition on account of space limitations are back where I want them. Our major annual events and celebrations are now included. An expanded index will be more helpful to the reader looking for categories of interest, from beaches to forgotten milldams. Suggestions for further reading have been updated.

There is also more inferential space between the lines of this new edition for the reader whose particular wants are broader or narrower, as the case may be, than the text is intended to meet. I mean, for example, the artist or photographer for whom this volume may offer the merest hint of some new vista, some hitherto undiscovered charm in a familiar scene.

The architecture, or art, or history, or maritime expert, or merely the enthusiast, may find one of the richest lodes anywhere, both in and between those lines.

Or there may be a mission, known only to himself, for the avocational botanist, cetologist, marine biologist, or geologist. How about an exploration of that interlinear world for the hiker, bird watcher, or berry picker, the sailor and the rower?

And for the inquisitive archeologist of the trivial, the poker-around, this old place offers more yard sales by the square foot and curiosity shops by the fathom than you can shake a broken oar at. Antiques and memorabilia? Why, half the town arises every weekday dawn to check the other half's rubbish put-out; a friend of mine thus rescued a slightly worn oriental rug, another a framed document signed by Thomas Jefferson.

But that's Gloucester.

The Gloucester Guide appeared in 1973 as one of four volumes published by Gloucester 350th Anniversary Celebration, Inc. After the shouting was over the unsold copies were purchased by Nelson B. Robinson, owner of Toad Hall Bookstore in Rockport, whose proprietress, Eleanor Hoy, distributed and sold them until the last was gone around 1987, when the rights were generously assigned to the author.

Like a Saint Joan of publishing, Laura Fillmore, president of Editorial Inc. in Rockport, came to the rescue in 1989 with the innovative notion of Protean (capable of great diversity) Press, a profit-sharing experiment in publishing "based on the something-from-nothing concept," as she put it, "inviting all who participate in the project to labor today for fruits tomorrow and the day after tomorrow."

So here is our first fruit, and the personal and professional pleasure has been protean in the cultivation thereof with production manager Fillmore, coordinator Marilyn Rash, copyeditor Jay Howland, designer Inga Soderberg, compositor Barbara Kassabian, proofreader David Alpher, salesperson David Eales, bookkeeper Herb Batten, and printer Dave McAveeney of The Pressroom.

J. E. G.
Black Bess, Eastern Point
January 1990

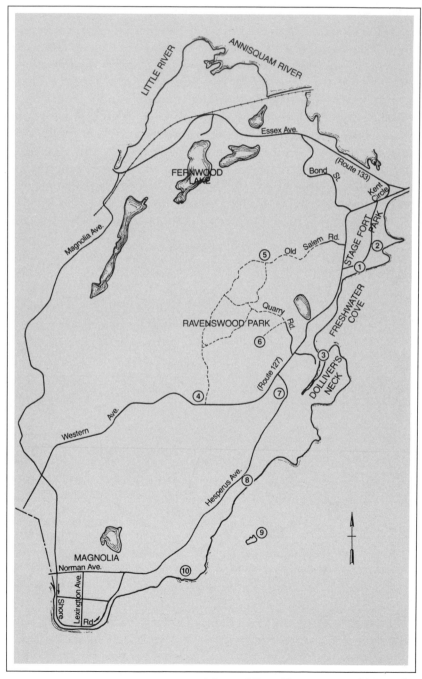

Map 1. West Gloucester and Magnolia

CHAPTER 1

WEST GLOUCESTER
AND MAGNOLIA

Stage Fort Park

A t Stage Fort Park, climb the twisting path up the stone steps to the highest elevation of Tablet Rock, the whaleback of granite that marks the first settlement of the Massachusetts Bay Colony at this spot in 1623, and take in the glorious view of Gloucester and its harbor.

What a harbor and what a history! There is the Atlantic to the south; to the west of that the North Shore; Eastern Point directly across; Ten Pound Island, and the old city, to the northeast. John Mason was making the first proper survey of the waterfront one autumn day when he dropped everything to take a count and ink it on his map: "1833 14 October four hundred and forty-three Vessels at anchor in the harbour besides what lay at Wharfs."

That was a hundred and fifty-six years ago, and two hundred and ten years after the fourteen men of the Dorchester Company landed at our feet, here from England to see if this fabulous New World they had heard such tales of would support a fishing and farming expedition. Look at the forested hills of West Gloucester behind you, and the rocks all around, and the pitiful soil of Fishermen's Field—and then back at this harbor again—and you will know in a flash how matters developed that John Mason counted four hundred and forty-three vessels out there, and why those fourteen failed, and why one of the organizers back in England, John White, would write it off thus: "First, that no sure fishing-place in the land is fit for planting, nor any good place for planting found fit for fishing; at least, near the shore: and, secondly, rarely any fisherman will work at land; neither are husbandmen fit for fishermen, but with long use and experience."

It was no use, short or long, and in 1626 Roger Conant led the First Fourteen men where the grass was greener, and started Salem. Then in 1631 a band of fishermen is believed to have settled at Annisquam, and that is probably the original site of the permanent settlement that was formally incorporated under The Reverend Richard Blynman in 1642.

This western shore of Gloucester never did prove to be much good for anything—except in olden times for scratching away at a dirt-starved little farm or two, for making shipwrecks and for launching lifeboats in the surf—for being caught in a suspension of life by the brush of Fitz Hugh Lane—for pleasure driving or sitting on the rocks looking asea, for building summer homes and castles, for swimming, picnicking, baseball games, ferris wheels and fireworks, dining, dancing under moonlight, shopping in very fancy shops, and variously disporting at a seaside so gentle and yet so defiant of the Atlantic swells that no ship ever found haven here except permanently. It is a coast for sea captains to retire to and for the rest of us to repair to when the soul needs the replenishment of the ocean and its breezes.

So here we are at Stage Fort Park, where there is ample public parking, a summer lunchstand, picnic grounds, a baseball field, and two public beaches: Cressy's (map 1, 1), the longer, facing south and named for former landholders, and Half Moon (map 1, 2), a jewel of a beach, a miniature nestled between the twin bluffs in the shade of the overhanging trees, forever a fresh discovery.

Somewhere on these grounds, as close as possible to the shore, those hardy, foolhardy adventurers pitched up their fishing stage and dried their first catches in 1623. A hundred and fifty years later, as insurance against British raiders from the sea, the Gloucester patriots built the breastwork on the north of Half Moon Beach, Stage Head.

When the mother country threatened her child again in the War of 1812, this fort was repaired, and two companies were stationed here. In the Civil War the fort was activated for the third time, as Fort Conant. And finally, not very seriously, during the Spanish War of 1898 the militia camped here a few weeks after the city had acquired the surrounding farm from the heirs of Benjamin K. Hough, thereby ending speculation that it might be subdivided into house lots.

The Houghs, father and son, appear to have been gentlemen farmers to some extent. The old man planted the big elms around 1850, and they allowed some run of their historic property. One summer when Buffalo Bill's troupe tented on the grounds his Indians discovered ancient Indian mounds here and made a singular impression on the curious townspeople with a ritual dance under the lead of their chief, in their bright-colored blankets and headdresses. The Spirit prevails, and traveling carnivals have encamped on the high ground of Stage Fort Park every summer for as long as the oldest resident can remember, and before that.

Freshwater Cove

Above Cressy's Beach we rejoin Western Avenue and travel this old North Shore road where once the Boston stagecoach bumped along. Almost immediately we are back above the harbor, overlooking Freshwater Cove, named for the spring Samuel de Champlain found here when he chanced upon "Le Beauport" in 1606.

Behind the masonry wall on our left is the property of The Reverend Moon's Unification Church, formerly the Cardinal Cushing Villa, a convalescent home, formerly Lookout Hill, the summer mansion of the late John Hays Hammond, Sr. Hammond was a Croesus of a mining engineer, a cohort of Cecil Rhodes in South Africa, and for a time on the Guggenheim family payroll at a salary reported to be a million dollars a year. He bought this estate perched on the cliff above the cove for $45,000 as a birthday present for his wife in 1906.

For some sixty years previously Lookout Hill had belonged to the Hovey family of Boston. The original house was built about 1845 as one of the earliest and costliest "cottages" on the North Shore by George O. Hovey, a Boston wholesale merchant and yachtsman who gathered up large tracts on the shore, including Dolliver's Neck and Mussel Point. Around 1847 his brother Charles, head of the Boston dry goods firm of C. H. Hovey and Company, built his own cottage up in town on Babson's Hill, a pasture above Pavilion Beach, where a street bears his name.

The Hovey brothers were probably the first out-of-towners to have summer homes in Gloucester. Their forerunners, however, were young merchant members of the Boston Pioneer Seashore Club, who brought the first organized camping-out parties to Gloucester around 1825. They used Charles Sawyer's fish houses at the Cove, tented on the shore, put on impromptu concerts for the locals, and flirted with the Cove Village girls. The Pioneers were succeeded by the ''999th Battery'' of Charlestown merchants, who brought concerts and lunches and salutes to dawn, noon, and sundown with blasts from their brass cannon.

Waterside Lane, a woodsy way across Western Avenue from Quarry Road, comes out to a high-tide public landing (map 1, 3) and a most delightful aspect of Freshwater Cove, its cozy channel to the harbor, its marshy reaches, and the former Coast Guard station across the tide on Dolliver's Neck.

George Hovey's neighbor on the south above the cove was Samuel E. Sawyer, who was born there in 1818 in Brookbank, the family homestead, and educated in Master Moore's school up the road. He departed for Boston at eighteen, made his fortune, and returned for fifty summers of his life, looking for ways to spend his money for the betterment of Gloucester.

Ravenswood Park

Sawyer was a dignified and fastidious gentleman who drove about Gloucester in an elegant turnout, with coachman up front behind a handsome prancing pair of horses. Before he died in 1889 he gave his fellow citizens, among other considerable benefactions, some three hundred endowed acres of forest above Western Avenue, to be called Ravenswood Park.

This purest of woodland preserves has steadily been enlarged by its trustees to around five hundred acres. Four or five miles of graded roads and paths have been cleared or created and a nondenominational chapel, for which Samuel Sawyer left funds, built at the entrance. As a result of foresight and careful stewardship, Ravenswood Park is the most accessible, extensive, and unspoiled forest on the North Shore. The main entrance is on Western Avenue half a mile beyond the junction with Hesperus Avenue at the Ravenswood Chapel and parking lot (map 1, 4), where a map of the paths is located. Automobiles are barred.

Ravenswood keeps its secrets for each new initiate, but we might mention that behind its magnificent stands of hardwood and evergreen it hides from all but the knowledgeable the wild magnolia, *Magnolia virginiana*. Here in the northwest swamp is its northernmost habitat.

A hundred years ago Historian Babson feared that the wholesale (and usually unsuccessful) attempts to transplant it would soon see the exotic shrub wiped out. It nearly was, but it is slowly coming back.

The Old Salem Road passes through the park and emerges on Western Avenue above Stage Fort. It was early called Old Pest House Road, being the site of the isolation hospital the town built for smallpox victims in 1777, during one of the epidemics that used to terrify people every few years. The site of the hut of Mason Walton, the gregarious "hermit" of Ravenswood who retreated here for his health and died in 1917 at seventy-nine, is marked on this road (map 1, 5). Walton wrote popular books and articles about his wildlife friends, walked sociably across the Cut for breakfast every morning, and was a kind of guru of his day for pilgrimages that dumped visitors by the thousands on his rustic stoop every year.

Quarry Road, off Western Avenue, incidentally, is another way into Ravenswood. We leave Quarry Road across from the entrance to Stillington Hall, the Buswell estate with its noted little theater and modern-day musicales, and strike off into the woods on the short trail to Ledge Hill, the high point of the western shore (map 1, 6). Around 1915, the Ravenswood trustees were going to put up a forty-foot observation

1. *Mason Walton, the self-styled Hermit of Gloucester, lived eighteen years in the wilds of Ravenswood, first in a tent, then in a log cabin; restored himself to health; and produced a classic of nature writing.*

tower but thought better of it. The view without it is enough and worth the climb.

Dolliver's Neck (Samuel Dolliver came down from Marblehead and bought a farm here in 1652) is the cradling arm of inner Freshwater Cove and was the Gloucester Coast Guard base from 1900, when the Treasury Department located the lifesaving service here on land given by the Hoveys, until it was moved to the inner harbor in 1973. Many a lifeboat rescue mission has put to sea from here, and many the foul-weather shore patrol has walked the coast as far as Kent Circle and Magnolia with lanterns to warn of disaster or discover it.

A tenth of a mile along Hesperus Avenue on the right-hand slope is the half-hidden little gambrel house of Master Joseph Moore (map 1, 7), the same who started Sam Sawyer on his way; years before Hesperus Avenue was laid, Master Moore's Lane stopped before his house and then evaporated into a path of colonial antiquity.

Master Moore was a lad of twelve when he and his father, William Moore, who built this house, were out fishing one fine August day of 1775 just as Captain John Lindsay came sailing around Eastern Point in the sloop of war *Falcon*. Lindsay had been chased away from the other side of the Cape, as we shall see, and had pursued a prize into the harbor, only to be routed again by the Gloucester patriots. His efforts to put the town to flames fared no better, and in a rage he came upon the peaceful Moores. The English commander captured the father for his pilot but left the boy to row ashore.

Joseph Moore never saw his sire again. Having a mathematical bent he took up teaching and kept school for sixty years, achieving a local fame through his book and his classes on navigation, which kept several generations of Gloucester skippers on their course.

Famously absentminded, Master Moore was leading his horse and old two-wheeled cart up Sawyer's Hill toward town one day when the fastening pin fell out. The body tilted and slid off the axle, but he trudged on unawares, lost in some navigational problem, until he met a surprised neighbor on the down slope who called out, ''Where are you going with your cartwheels, Master Moore?''

''Eh, what cartwheels? Why, bless me! I started from home with a cart. I must have left part of it somewhere on the road!''

Mrs. Theodora Codman bequeathed to the Massachusetts Audubon Society as a sanctuary twenty-five acres of Moore woodland west of

Hesperus Avenue, open to the public, and her estate on the shore, which can be visited by appointment.

Hammond Museum

A half a mile beyond Master Moore's house on Hesperus Avenue is the medieval castle—yes, the castle—of the late John Hays Hammond, Jr., brilliant and eccentric son of the engineer (map 1, 8). Like his father's Lookout Hill, this astounding creation—"Abbadia Mare" (Abbey-by-the-Sea)—went to the Roman Catholic Archdiocese of Boston on his death in 1965 and is now owned by a nonprofit corporation.

Jack Hammond startled Gloucester on the eve of World War I by scooting a passengerless boat around the harbor via remote radio control from his laboratory. This was the dramatic overture of his pioneering inventions in radio, radar, television, and frequency modulation, which spilled over into all kinds of fields with more than eight hundred patents.

The most flamboyant of Hammond's extraordinary works is this castle, which he built on the bluff above the ocean for his home, his laboratory, his expanding art collection, and his multitubinous pipe organ (he had nothing to do with the electric organ of the same name). Hammond was fascinated with the bizarre and the gothic, and he loved to amaze, so his castle is a potpourri of the odd, the romanesque, the medieval, the Renaissance, all strangely dovetailed—a Roman bath, artificial rain, secret passages and peepholes, a great pseudocathedral hall a hundred feet long and sixty feet high to show off the colossal organ he designed with some 10,000 pipes—and in a courtyard patio, turned modestly toward the sea, a statue of himself in the buff.

An odd genius, Jack Hammond built his castle between 1925 and 1928 mostly, though the organ took twenty years. Concerts are given on it regularly. The museum has a full schedule of year-round events and is open daily 9:00 to 5:00.

Norman's Woe and Rafe's Chasm

From a lofty parapet of Hammond Castle you can look directly south on the hulking, guano-smeared gull roost of Norman's Woe Rock (map 1, 9). If it's a day when the mountainous swells of a dying easterly storm are rolling in and devastating themselves on the rocks eighty feet below, each successive sea will double its height in an explosion of spray on this dire ledge. Though many a vessel has come to grief on Norman's Woe, Henry Longfellow's imagined protagonist was not among them, and the poet never laid eyes on the rock until years after he wrecked the *Hesperus* on it. Who Norman was, and why so woeful, nobody knows. On a still, moonlit night, when a slow swell is undulating onto shore, there is no music to the ears like the distant careless clanging of the bell buoy that warns mariners to keep clear.

A shade over six-tenths of a mile beyond the Hammond Museum is a parking turnoff and a path leading to the shore through the city's Rafe's Chasm Reservation (map 1, 10). Originally Rafe's "Crack," it's said to have been named for a "Ralph" living in the area. The chasm is a prodigious split in the ledge some two hundred feet long, ten feet across at its greatest width, and sixty feet deep; the seas roar in with terrific detonations, and countless of the curious who ventured into it, or merely verged too close, have been flicked off and drowned. The broad ledges to the west are open to the public and well worth a picnic party. Motorists should lock up and leave nothing valuable behind.

Magnolia

Hesperus Avenue becomes Norman Avenue and we enter the last domain of Gloucester's western shore, an area known many years ago as Knowlton's Point, for the people who farmed here, but since the late 1860s, when the first summer boarders discovered it, as Magnolia.

2. *Heading north on the west shore of Magnolia Point, Shore Road was Lobster Lane in 1890, Crescent Beach behind the fishermen's shacks.*

3. *The Perkins House for summer boarders in Magnolia was the nucleus of The Oceanside in the 1870s. Look at the odds and ends of Union Army uniforms on the fellows at right.*

Magnolia today is a residential village and a far cry from the exclusive resort that for fifty years—until World War II—was the swinging social center of the North Shore. It all started when Daniel Fuller moved down from Swampscott in 1868 to a large piece of farm on the point (only farmers and shore fishermen here then) and built a few summer cottages. Ten years later he opened the Hesperus House for a hundred guests, quite fashionable, on the north side of Hesperus Avenue between Lexington Avenue and Fuller Street.

All in a rush Magnolia became *the* place to go to on the North Shore in that gilded age when the wealthy packed the whole family, along with forty-three trunks, maids, pets, carriage or auto, and coachman or chauffeur, off to a very proper resort for the summer in a Victorian railroad station of a hotel surrounded by miles of piazzas and acres of lawns, tennis courts, croquet fields, and putting greens.

The most splendid of them all was The Oceanside, next block east on Hesperus Avenue from The Hesperus. George Upton started with a two-story boardinghouse in 1879, and when he sold out in 1908 for over a half a million dollars, he had a sprawling establishment of six hundred rooms, ten nearby cottages, a dining room a hundred and fifty by forty-five feet, a casino with a black ceiling studded with starlike electric globes, and exactly eight hundred and eighty-one feet of piazza. Five more years, and The Oceanside had absorbed The Hesperus as an annex, had spawned another dozen cottages and a hundred and fifty more rooms, and was the biggest resort hotel in New England.

Ambassadors, royalty, multimillionaires, presidential confidants, the great and the aspiring from the world over flocked to The Oceanside and the other hotels of Magnolia to be seen, to play, to dance at the extravagant balls, to watch the horse shows and gymkhanas on Crescent Beach, to athleticize, to romance, to conspire, and to eye the next rung on the ladder of society.

4. *Magnolia's Oceanside in its glory, the biggest summer hotel in New England.*

Today scarcely a trace is left. The Hesperus burned around 1950, and The Oceanside followed in 1958. Only a glimmer of the glamor of Lexington Avenue remains where once along the colonnades and under the arcades the summer branches of the spiffiest shops in America made ''Robbers' Row''—as some of their clientele ungenerously called it—the spending mecca north of Boston. An ice cream parlor occupies the site of the Town Grille, later Del Monte's, on the southeast corner of Lexington and Norman, where the smart set partied the night away, and the street was lined with waiting chauffeurs. Gone is The Casino on the shore behind Rafe's Chasm, where the jazz of Ruby Newman and Sammy Eisen kept the debutante parties alive all night, and scrambled eggs were served as the sun exploded up out of the sea.

But the sea remains, and Magnolia keeps her charms. Norman Avenue ends at Crescent, or Gray, Beach and the public landing, with ramp and small parking lot, below the firehouse where Shore Road begins. From here we catch the sweep of Manchester's tony beach, where the sports raced their horses over the hard sand before the first World War. Coolidge Point is beyond, and then, to sea, barren Great Egg Rock, and Kettle Island and the narrows where the fishermen set their traps for the migrating mackerel.

Shore Road is one-way past the stubs of the pier where the excursion steamers touched in the heyday. (The neighbors once got so mad at the litter left by the day-trippers from the old SS *Empire State* that they tore up the planking of the wharf.) The narrow, surf-splashed road gives a grand panorama of ocean as it rims the shore estates. At the final bend there is a place to hold up and look beyond the rusty ledges of Norman's Woe Point, clear across the entrance of Gloucester Harbor to the outer end of Eastern Point, an intriguing hint of all that lies inside. Then Shore Road joins Hesperus Avenue, and we dive into the Magnolia woods so thick and lush in midsummer that they look and smell and feel like a semitropical rain forest.

The Little Heater

The junction of Magnolia and Western avenues was one corner of the "Little Heater" when the hoss was boss, a rough triangle of three roads that was far and away the most popular drive for the smart turnouts, carriages, buggies, pacers, teams, matched pairs, and horseback riders of the resort era. No one is quite sure how Magnolia Avenue to Essex Avenue at Little River to Western Avenue at Kent Circle and back to Magnolia Avenue, or the reverse, got such a name. Some say because it warmed up your horses; others because it was shaped like a snowplow called a heater; others because it resembled in outline a chunk of cast iron, a heater, which the housewife heated on the stove before dropping in the hollow of her flatiron; and still others because it was a "heat" for the gents who savored racing their fast trotters around it. There was a "Big Heater" too, a longer trot along Essex Avenue to Essex, south on Southern Avenue and School Street to Manchester, returning to Kent Circle by Magnolia Avenue.

5. *The icehouse of the Fernwood Lake Ice Company, the largest in Massachusetts, capacity 34,000 tons, supplied the greatest fishing fleet in the world a hundred years ago.*

The Little Heater takes us north on Magnolia Avenue through the dense Magnolia woods and swamp, cool on a hot day under the arching trees. We give the horses their head past Kondelin Road and the industrial park; we rein them in for the zigzag turn under the railroad overpass and beside the tracks by the water filtration plant, Essex Avenue and Little River up ahead. (Avoid the junction when the cars are due, cautioned an 1896 guidebook. "If you have a spirited horse an unpleasant experience might be yours should you meet the train.")

Now we're out of the woods, and Little River stretches lazily out before us through its marshes. This is a high-tide public landing. The Lily Pond, which the train runs by (a lovely, secluded gem up at the end of Laurel Street, off Essex Avenue), overflows along the roadbed to this estuary of Squam River, where the settler Jacob Davis built a sawmill in 1682. His son is probably responsible for the restored colonial house at the bend in the road. Tradition has it that when the British tried to land on Peter Coffin's beach on an August day in 1775, Robert, one of his slaves, saved his master's life and was freed for it, taking from that moment the surname of Freeman and this land and house as a gift. However it came about, generations of Freemans lived in the old place until the last of the line, Hattie Johnson, died here in 1931 at the age of eighty-one. For some years the house was an inn, and mine host enjoyed informing weary travelers that "it's seven miles to Gloucester and every mile uphill"—or so it seemed.

Three-quarters of the first uphill mile of Essex Avenue going east (the second side of the Little Heater) cuts inland of Stanwood Point, a place originally of summer camps a hundred and fifteen years ago, strung along on slopes brown with pine needles above Little River. Barnard Stanwood advertised in 1869 that he had "recently fitted up a new grove at West Gloucester near the head of Little River and within ten rods of the depot—for picnics—thirty acres pine and oak—plenty water—platform 50 x 30 feet roofed over for dancing." Off Stanwood Avenue on the left of the unpaved parking area is a high-tide public landing.

Past Fernwood Lake, well-carved granite posts on the right invite us up the hill, where Sonolite's factory now occupies the foundations of the biggest icehouse in Massachusetts, put there by Francis W. Homans in 1876; it was two hundred and thirty-six by two hundred and ten feet, with a capacity of 34,000 tons, which is a lot of ice. Homans was a smart Yankee who saw a way to reduce the price of ice to the Gloucester fishing industry, and he established a practical monopoly by erecting his enormous shed and then making the pond to fill it from. It was merely a matter of dredging the swamp and damming the stream, and he had Fernwood Lake.

Add to this another picnic grove on the west shore of Fernwood, and canoes for hire, and the swains of Gloucester and Essex had a place to take their girls on a summer evening by trolley from either town before the motor car drove it off the tracks in 1920.

A quarter of a mile farther on toward Gloucester on Essex Avenue is the Squam River plant built by the Russia Cement Company, which concocted Le Page's glue out of Gloucester's fish skins. When the wind was from the west the distinctive emanations from the company's tall chimney assured the town that all was well and working "over to the Russia." Le Page's made its own pond, dubbed by the youngsters who skated on it "The Banjo" for its shape, and—needing more fresh water for the mysterious process of converting fish to glue—built another around 1907 next to Fernwood Lake.

The road to the city, advised a cyclist's handbook of 1885, "is sadly out of repair, due, in great measure, to the heavy teaming of the ice company, which is almost constant over it."

Today it is tires by the thousands, and we hum back over the well-traveled causeway along the marsh to Kent Circle and the salt breeze of the harbor, completing the Little Heater and our tour of West Gloucester "over the Cut."

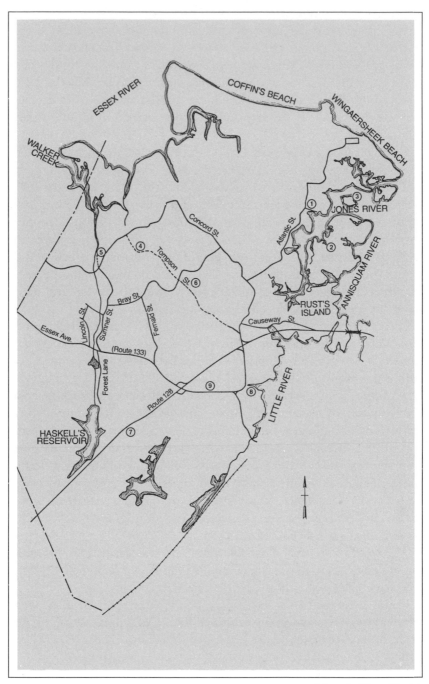

Map 2. West Parish

CHAPTER 2

WEST PARISH

West Parish was first defined as an ecclesiastical subdivision of Gloucester, and this countryish name has stuck with it, although even some of the natives aren't sure just where it is. They will agree, though, that along with Dogtown up in the heart of the Cape, the forests, ponds, streams, salt marshes, dunes, and gleaming beaches that make up the territory west of the Annisquam and Little rivers and Magnolia Avenue are Gloucester's back country. How long West Parish will remain so in the face of avid and determined developers depends upon the resolution of the community as a whole.

Evidently the English immigrants who took grants of land in this backwash a mile and a half from the harbor had no great taste for the sea; otherwise, why would they and their progeny put up with seventy-five years of hiking and rowing an ungodly number of miles every Sunday to attend compulsory meeting across the river at the Green? But finally they had enough of it, and in one of the first successful acts of rebellion in the colonies, they seceded from the First Parish, hired a pastor, and built a meetinghouse in 1716. Second, or West, Parish it remains today after two hundred and seventy-three years.

It is sleepy country. Even the sea comes in softly. Rip Van Winkle could wake up here and turn over for another forty winks.

Originally the Second Parish was everything west of the Annisquam ("Squam") and Little rivers and a straight line from the head of the latter to the Manchester line at Kettle Cove; for practical purposes today that line could be bent along Magnolia Avenue.

Except for the Coffin family farm in back of their great beach, West Parish was a wilderness in the early days. There were no more than three or four passable roads. These survive today in various degrees of passability, and they have been joined by surprisingly few others.

Most of the wilderness survives too, as we shall see, and the beaches, dunes, marshes, streams, and inlets. The clock has by no means stopped in West Parish, yet this remains the part of Cape Ann that looks and sounds and even smells the oldest and least altered by man. It has the elements of a fading colonial preserve.

This is the least familiar part of town, save to the people here, who like it that way. West Parish keeps to itself. Many the Squammer or Rocky Necker isn't sure quite how to get here, though with a little prompting he could find Coffin's Beach, where he recalls going on his high school graduation picnic.

To observe the standoffishness of West Parish and the islandishness of Gloucester proper, pause in the parking turnoff on the westbound side of the Route 128 bridge named for the late A. Piatt Andrew, the city's only resident U.S. congressman. From this height the Annisquam River is a moat twisting between the gentle marshes and the cottaged shore from Gloucester Harbor to Ipswich Bay. Almost directly below, looking southward from the eastbound turnout, West Parishioners for a hundred years were ferried between Biskie Head of Rust's Island on our right and Trynall Cove across the river. Until this span was built after World War II, the drawbridge at the Cut provided the only road connection between the two parts of Gloucester.

Heading west over the Route 128 bridge, bear right beyond the overpass on the old causeway that got West Parishioners to Rust's Island and the Squam River ferry. Today the causeway traverses the "Window on the Marsh," a mere two acres—but, had one more factory or automobile showroom gone in here, it would have ruined the view of a clear two-mile stretch of salt grass and river. The window was purchased through a public fund drive and given to the Essex County Greenbelt Association for safekeeping.

Almost directly across from the Window on the Marsh, incidentally—off Route 128 eastbound—is the Stoney Cove Reservation acquired by Greenbelt in 1979, a window on Little River from the long stone pier that juts over the salt marsh from the small parking area. This was the mainland terminus of the colonial ferry, and barges a hundred years ago left here at high water, loaded with granite from the West Parish quarries.

A path marked and maintained by Greenbelt rises and falls and ducks in and out of the woods on Susan's and Presson's points, with glimpses and overviews of the flats of Squam and Little rivers. When a high-course tide laps the south shore of Presson's Point, out from the water breeches a granite whale, jaws as joyfully open as his famous, now-fractured cousin up on Dogtown.

Resuming our westward course back across Route 128 at the end of Causeway Street, we turn right on Concord Street, the old Round-the-Parish Road, and are on our way.

Jones River

Concord Street shies away from the marshes, but we want to visit them and the great beach beyond, so we part company after three-quarters of a mile and swing to the right on Atlantic Street. After a short distance the road suddenly emerges on the edge of what the map identifies grandiosely as Jones River, better known as Jones Creek because it drains to mostly flats and swarms of voracious midsummer midges and greenhead flies at low water.

The right way to survey this prairie of salt marsh is to get plonked down in the middle of it, which we do just short of a mile along Atlantic Street by turning onto a stone pier that spears a quarter of a mile across the marsh to the edge of the creek itself (map 2, 1). This is a high-tide public landing with a ramp and small parking lot.

Here is midmarsh. To the east, across the creek and the undulating grasses, is the wooded backside of Pearce's, once Millet's and sometimes known as Merchant's, Island, which harbors a tight little summer colony in Farmer Merchant's meadow on the Squam River shore (map 2, 2). While the big river itself is out of sight, we can trace its course by the summer cottages that hang on its steep banks from Squam to Ferry Hill. On our left is the lesser knoll of Ram Island (map 2, 3) and at our backs the beginning of the West Parish woods. It is three-quarters of a mile between the shores of the Squam River basin where we are. The two-mile length of it, including Jones Creek, is a fertile, teeming spawning ground and nursery for the life of the ocean, the life of the marsh itself of course, and the life of the nearby land.

The Long Stone Pier is all that's left of the scheme of a speculator around 1880, who is said to have spent so much money blasting the granite from the hill across the road back there and building a place for sloops to sail in and take on the stone that he went broke before he was ever close to producing a paying block of paving. This lonely spot was busy enough forty-five years later, though; more booze changed hands on Prohibition midnights than granite ever did.

Far from the pollution of the earth and the distant signs of habitation and sounds of traffic, the marsh and the islands and the shore here look as they must always have, their inner life presided over by the raucous crows and wheeling bank swallows and the silent, baleful, black-crowned heron of the night.

The Beaches

On to the beach.

Along Atlantic Street the windswept, sanded-over woods shrink to scrub oak, sumac, wild cherry, and cedar. Ahead are the private roads of the Wingaersheek summer colony and Coffin's Beach on Ipswich Bay. Turning right for the city-owned Wingaersheek Beach, we pop out upon a desert world of sand: bleached mounds and hillocks and mountains of it to make the eyes squint, here and there a barely subsisting juniper, the dunes tufted tenaciously with the toughest grass

6. *Wingaersheek Beach in the 1890s, somebody's summer tent way off there. From behind these dunes Peter Coffin and his men bluffed off Captain Lindsay's landing party in 1775.*

in creation, the baking parking lot, and then the smooth, shining, shimmering slope of the beach. This is the summit of the underwater mountain of sand that shifts restlessly and endlessly where the currents of the bay meet the pliant land and make the treacherous shoals, the beaches, the entrance to Squam River—and remake them and unmake them.

Take to the beach and look across the channel to Annisquam and its lighthouse, as close as if they were handpainted on china. Then walk to the southeast end of the beach and trace the river's retreat, or the ocean's penetration, into the marsh that keeps West Parish to itself. Come here and share the scene with the sandpipers and the gulls, and the terns dipping into the surf if it's a hard easterly, and imagine how it was that fifth of August in 1775 when the English *Falcon* stood in Squam Channel there and Captain Lindsay sent fifty men in a barge for mutton from Farmer Peter Coffin's pasture.

Mustering a handful of his men, including a slave or two, our major of militia took a position behind these dunes and set up such a crackling of musketry that the Redcoats hastily put about without touching the beach, supposing they were faced with a company at least—their fear magnified by the shouts of tailor Robbins, borne on the wind: ''Wheel by battalions! Fire by generations!''

Not far behind the dunes stood the farmhouse of the Coffins for generations and the building where they housed their slaves. All traces of these, and indeed of the farm and its fine stand of trees, disappeared long before the Civil War. There is a tale that on his deathbed the old hero enjoined his sons to preserve the woods on the property as they would the grass that holds the dunes in place—but they tired of agriculture and cut and sold the timber for a quick profit, and the drifting sand took over.

The origin of the name ''Wingaersheek,'' which its promoters gave to their summer colony at the east end of Coffin's Beach in the 1890s, remains a mystery. Historian Babson thought it was the Indian name for Cape Ann, while James Pringle suggested that it might be a corruption of the Dutch ''Wyngaerts Hoeck,'' a land abounding in grapes.

For a mile and a half from Farm Point, Coffin's Beach arches elegantly, and an elegant hike it is, out and back, the clean sand drifting off so gently that a mile offshore the bay is only twenty feet deep. Around 1888 a Buffalo lawyer named Edward C. Hawks bought the

Coffin farm and built "Hawksworth Hall" of granite quarried nearby, barged to the beach and dragged up to the site by oxen. Later his brother, James D. Hawks, Detroit railroad tycoon, who planted 10,000 Austrian pines on the dunes, reclaimed some of the 1,000 acres he accumulated and built his own castle, "The Bungalow," at the east end of the beach. In 1924 his widow donated Wingaersheek Beach to the city, and cottages since have been erected the entire length of the dunes.

Beyond Two Penny Loaf at the west end of the beach, the tides swirl through the shifting mouth of the Essex River; across, the beach resumes at Castle Neck. Farm Creek insinuates itself behind Coffin's and waters the marsh that makes Coles Island, saved from development in 1989 by a local group of environmentally conscious investors.

Back on Concord Street, the "Round-the-Parish Road" plunges through the woods for another mile beyond Atlantic Street until once again, veering sharply to the left, we're in old saltwater farm country. Along here the road plays hide-and-seek with Essex Bay, quiet and unhurried, past homes settled on their foundations for two hundred years and more, their dooryards basking in the southern exposure that seems to favor roses, daylilies, and hollyhocks. The road avoids ledges but climbs Heartbreak Hill of imperceptible elevation. Without warning the brush suddenly parts to reveal a couple of miles straight out of marsh and salt river that carry the eye to the crest of Ipswich's Hog (Choate) Island, only to flash shut again to the intimacy of a country lane.

Walker Creek

West another half a mile along Concord Street is another surprise, Walker Creek. This capillary of tide wends north through a broadening swath of salt marshes, snakes around Tommy Island, insinuates into Essex, and by Conomo Point unites with the Essex River. South from the wooden bridge here the tide exhausts its momentum in the denseness of the vale between Sumner and Lincoln Streets, turns brackish, and at last loses the uphill battle of the waters altogether to Haskell's Brook.

The creek is the site of one of the first tidal mills in the New World (map 2, 5). The mill's foundation is on private property whose owner

7. Haskell's grist mill at Walker Creek was on its last legs in the 1890s. So was Dobbin.

permits visitors if they leave the place as they found it. The access is a tenth of a mile back from the creek on Concord Street, down the old cart track that comes out from the brush onto a bulge of large stones and fill, the base of the mill. The remains of the dam, some rocks and waterlogged timbers, are evident at low tide. The view down the creek from here is one of the reasons why West Parish wants to stay West Parish.

William and Mark Haskell had the license of the town in 1690 to build this tide mill for grinding corn. The dam was high enough then to make a pond of every incoming tide by means of floodgates (and with the help of the brook); the controlled outflow turned the water-wheel that turned the stones. Vessels are said to have docked here to take on meal for the West Indies trade, although there seems hardly enough depth for any but the smallest craft; perhaps they were lighters or gundalows.

The pasture on the rise across Concord Street from the mill was used during the Civil War as a training ground by a Danvers company of

8. In the years after the Civil War entire families took to summer tenting, as on the Presson farm in the 1870s, presumably on Presson's Point beside Little River.

soldiers. One hot day in the middle of summer their captain marched them down to the creek at high tide and off the mill dam, in columns.

Tompson Street

Tompson Street, the street of ghosts, is vagrant and elusive but worth pursuit. It requires a digression from our circuit ride of the parish. We take Sumner Street along the upper reaches of Walker Creek, then go left on Bray Street, a winding, woodsy road. A short distance in to the right, a side trip down Fernald Street leaves civilization momentarily behind for a veritable black forest, the "Dark Hole," bottoming out around the base of Slough Hill and described by a writer in 1892 as "beautiful and attractive from the very neglect to which it has been left." The Dark Hole emerges into the daylight of Essex Avenue. How long it will remain dark is a question: a developer in 1989 had plans to build two hundred and seventy-nine homes and a golf course on three hundred and fifty-seven acres of wilderness and wetland between Route 128, Essex Avenue, and Fernald, Bray, and Tompson streets.

Eight-tenths of a mile west of Sumner Street, where Bray bends to the left past a charming old homestead, Tompson Street creeps across the road.

North, on our left, this remnant of a colonial way descends and weaves along between lichened stone walls piled high and close on either hand, hardly a rock displaced after two hundred and sixty-five years. Deep into the wilderness of West Parish we follow this sylvan and timeless path. It keeps company with a gurgling stream for a while, and fords it, and emerges at an ancient, stone-walled cemetery on our right, the Second Parish Burial Ground. On this long-deserted road named after their first pastor, The Reverend Samuel Tompson (map 2, 4), the West Parishioners located their 1716 meeting house and the second oldest graveyard in Gloucester.

The burial ground was a clear plot of slope then, bounded cleanly by its wall and open to the sky. The wall was not high enough to stop the forest or the desecrators. Nevertheless, a few monuments or fragments have survived; the careful engraving across some of these gray slates is as clean as the day it was cut by a hand turned to dust two hundred and seventy years ago.

Time seems in suspension as one passes one's fingertips over the earliest discernible death's-head, which marks the remains of Sarah, wife of John Tyler. She died at nineteen years and eleven months on February 22, 1720, exactly twelve years to the day before the birth of George Washington. Deacon Josiah Choate died in 1798 at eighty-three. He has two stones fore and aft, a giant oak now rising up between; was there an acorn in his pocket when they planted him?

Off to one side, as if deferentially, until recent years was a tall slab in the speckled shade with the words: ''Ye BODY OF Ye REVd Mr. SAMUEL TOMPSON PASTOUR OF Ye 2d CHURCH OF CHRIST IN GLOSESTER AGED 33 YEARS DEC DECEMBER YE 8 1724.'' They said of this young graduate of Harvard, who survived only eight years of the wilderness where they buried him, that ''he was of a pleasant aspect and mien; of a sweet temper; inoffensive in his whole behavior; pious and peaceable in his conversation.'' Here he rests, passably peaceable after two hundred and sixty-five years, but now unmarked—his stone carried off by one less pious and less inoffensive.

Back at Bray Street, if we were to ascend the remains of Tompson Street where it crosses to the south, we would be climbing Meetinghouse Hill. This isn't much of a hill, but it's enough in two hundred and fifty yards to open to view the grassy clearing on our left where the church was built in 1716 (map 2, 6). There was a time when you could look clear across to the sea from here. But the woods have grown up. Long after the old church gave way to its successor on the road to Essex in 1833 the stout oak edifice stood here, until in 1846 it was dismantled and rearranged as Liberty Hall on Essex Avenue, just south of the present junction with Route 128. After serving as fire station, branch library, polling place, and dance hall, the sacred timbers of Liberty Hall were finally dispersed when the road was widened for automobile traffic.

A stone altar put here by the West Gloucester Trinitarian Congregational Church marks the site of the original church. On training days the West Parishioners drilled to arms in front of their meetinghouse, and after they fell out probably fell in again at the tavern down the road on the left; its foundation was still evident years ago, and there may be a stone or two left if one knew where to search. Southward, Tompson Street makes its leisurely way between its walls (for it has nowhere to go any longer) through the light woods, over hill and dale. Low-bush blueberries creep to the edge of the hard ruts, worn in places to the bare ledge that still shows the scars of iron-rimmed cart wheels. Lot walls lose themselves in the thicket where half-hidden rosebushes guard granite doorsteps like dogs at the graves of their departed masters.

A few houses toward the end of the street justify the sign that preserves the name if not the memory of Pastor Tompson. The road rejoins Concord Street. Across is an abandoned drive-in theater, site of a controversial projected shopping mall. So ends, or begins, a once-traveled parish road. Through a mile and a quarter of wilderness it's inhabited today by none but the Haskells and the Riggses, the Tylers, old Deacon Choate, the Herricks and the Brays, who reside in their burial ground under the eternal ministry of pleasant, sweet-tempered pastor. But for how long?

Haskell's Brook

Having finished with Tompson Street, we return to our point of digression, where Bray departed Sumner Street, and continue to race Walker Creek upstream as it merges with Haskell's Brook until we strike Essex Avenue (Route 133). The brook rushes under the highway here through a gorge between Sumner and Lincoln streets; the road in fact was built on the sawmill dam erected before 1690 by William Haskell, the settler for whom the stream was named. The stone base of the mill and the dam can still be seen in the ravine. The Haskells who constructed the tide mill downstream at Walker Creek were no doubt the sons of this doughty pioneer.

Deacon Haskell's house has survived better than his mill; it stands a tenth of a mile down the brook on Lincoln Street, well shaded, on the right. Haskell bought it in 1652 from Richard Window, probably the builder. There have been additions, but the core structure is in good condition. It is privately owned.

Forest Lane, across the highway, follows upstream by Deacon Haskell's mill pond, greatly reduced in size since it drove his water wheel as recently as a hundred and fifteen years ago; in winter it's a skating rink. The forest hereabouts rang and crashed with the clamor of axes and falling trees, echoed to the shouts of the woodcutters and the thump of logs behind the straining oxen, screamed to the shrills of Haskell's buzz saw slicing this big timber into lumber for the houses and the vessels of Cape Ann, Salem, and Boston—for lumbering was the mainstay industry here before the virgin stands gave out and the men turned to the sea.

Forest Lane leads to the pumping station and dam of Haskell's Brook Reservoir, scooped from the swamp in 1901–03 by the Gloucester Water Supply Company as its fourth such project. Dike's Meadow, actually a swamp half a mile east of Haskell's, and Wallace Brook, south of Little River, were both dammed in the 1880s to make one hundred and thirty acres of water and over five hundred and eighty of watershed, while a five-million-gallon pressure storage reservoir was built on top of Bond's Hill behind Stage Fort Park. By 1885, Gloucester boasted "an inexhaustible source of pure water" running off the forest floor primeval of West Parish—a considerable overstatement.

Mount Ann

Mount Ann Park (map 2, 7) is owned by the Trustees of Reservations. The summit is a baldish plateau of ledge that the glacier carelessly strewed with boulders, as it did almost everything else in the wake of its retreat from Cape Ann. If the day is extra clear we can glimpse the Atlantic and a bend of Squam River and a bit of dune to the north.

Though at two hundred and seventy-two feet this is the top of Cape Ann, the view is not what it once was before the trees grew up; one hundred and twenty-five years ago Historian Babson could make out Wachuset, Monadnock, Gunstock, and Agamenticus mountains from the summit—and Bunker Hill Monument in Charlestown.

Mount Ann's old name is Tompson Mountain, the highest in a wooded "range" that also bears the pastor's name and extends from the southwest to the northeast of us as Tompson Mountain, Hardy Mountain, Lawrence Mountain, and Slough Hill. This range runs true to Cape Ann's arresting topography, rippled northeast-southwest by ribs and trenches in the ledge that make the marshy inlets for the sea and the inland gullies we've dammed for our fresh water supply. This washboard may have been created by the shifting and shearing of the earth's crust when it was cooling off.

Cape Ann's highest peak is most easily reached up the steep, broad path from the least accessible point of departure, the fenced-off and abandoned parking lot off the eastbound lane of Route 128.

Fishermen's Rest

We come full cycle on the Round-the-Parish Road by driving east on Route 128 a mile and a quarter and once again joining Concord Street. South this time, it takes us by Presson's Point and Kent's Cove, a pretty inlet of Little River (map 2, 8). Kent's Cove has an intimate charm. On its south bank is a high-tide public landing reached by a partially overgrown right of way from Concord Street, seventy-five yards west of the culvert through which the brook trickles under the road to the cove.

Concord Street comes out on Essex Avenue. The right turn, going west back toward 128, brings us in a quarter of a mile to the city's Beechbrook Cemetery (map 2, 9). The section at the entrance is the Gloucester Fishermen's Rest, the gift of the Cape Ann Fisherman's Home in 1920.

A beautiful and touching place. Row upon row of simple headstones answer to the roll of Gloucester's men of the sea who lived to die ashore. Anchors from the fishing vessels are buried with them, their white shanks the sentinel corner posts where the graveled walks meet.

Among the legion here is Howard Blackburn, Gloucester's heroic dory-man and lone voyager. Reads the inscription on a stone beside his:

> Many an angry sea they fought
> Their lives and vessels to save
> Their courage won what they sought
> An escape from a watery grave.

Reads another:

> Their decks were awash fore and aft
> Their sails were torn to a shred.
> Masts and spars were all adrift
> But here they lie, not in ocean bed.

Gazing upon these hundreds of markers arrayed in rank and file, one has the feeling of a military cemetery, as if all here had made common cause—as indeed they did. Engraved on another monument:

> These lads have joined the silent majority and lie here in peace. Where no wind or wave can disturb their rest. Charmed by the sea they fought many a gale with a courage and fortitude typical of Gloucester fishermen.

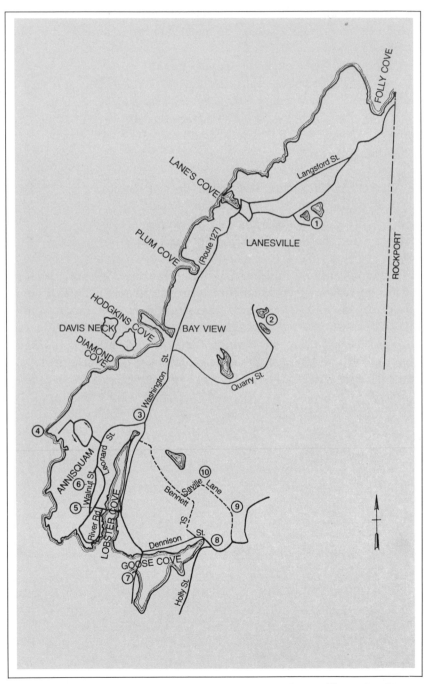

FOLLY COVE

LANE'S COVE

Langsford St.

LANESVILLE

①

ROCKPORT

PLUM COVE

(Route 127)

BAY VIEW

②

HODGKINS COVE

DAVIS NECK

DIAMOND COVE

Washington St.

Quarry St.

③

④

ANNISQUAM

Leonard St.

⑩

Saville Lane

Bennett St.

Walnut St.

⑥

River Rd.

LOBSTER COVE

⑤

⑨

Dennison St.

⑧

GOOSE COVE

⑦

Holly St.

Map 3. Lanesville to Annisquam

CHAPTER 3

LANESVILLE
TO ANNISQUAM

For about twenty-five years, much too brief a chapter in our history, the outlying villages of Cape Ann were connected by a street railway before it was abandoned for the buses in 1920. In the rattling good days of the trolleys you could travel from New York to Gloucester by way of Essex, West Parish, and the Cut, for a penny a mile. From the Waiting Station (now the bus stop) on Main Street, branch lines took you to Rocky Neck, or over the trestle in the windy observation cars to Long Beach, the local version of Revere Beach. Or you could go out Eastern Avenue and along the Nugent Stretch past Webster's Field, where thousands piled off the cars and the trains for the semipro baseball games of the New England League. Or on to Rockport, swaying above the sea at places, and back through Pigeon Cove, Lanesville, Bay View, Annisquam, and Riverdale to the Waiting Station.

The electric trolley cars are long gone, but the route is still there, and the sudden view of Folly Cove from the bend past Halibut Point is always a fresh surprise. If a northwest breeze has blown away the haze, Ipswich Bay sparkles off to the thin line of New Hampshire.

Folly Cove

Most of Folly Cove is in Gloucester. Years ago a village of dory fishermen hauled their boats out on the rocks here. Their gear shacks had a grip on the southern shore above the storm's reach; the quarry industry later built a pier from which the stone sloops could take on granite. There is a public landing down the footpath where the highway approaches closest to the shore. Upstream of the marsh behind the cove was a mill. The mill dam is said to exist somewhere in the thicket back there; but the shacks have gone, the mill has gone, the quarry pits are silent, and Folly Cove is a symbolic introduction to Gloucester's bold Ipswich Bay shore, where the fishing and the farming are pursued now avocationally if at all, and quarrying, lumbering, milling, shipbuilding, foreign trade, coasting, and all other industries but lobstering are history.

Folly Cove's given name is Gallop's Folly, in sardonic memory of John Gallop, a Boston pilot who had the bad luck to pile up a ship here in 1635. It would be folly indeed to seek haven at this place in dirty weather with a sea making up. And many a scuba diver has drowned in its treacherous waters.

Lanesville sprawls along the granite from here to the south shore of Plum Cove, but its heart is its harbor, Lane's Cove, which was Flatstone Cove until soon after John Lane settled there in 1704. Day fishing in Ipswich Bay remains Lanesville's oldest industry. Its richest, however, fished chunks of granite from the depths of the ledge. Quarries lasted for only seventy-five years, not because the supply gave out but because asphalt and concrete replaced paving blocks and building stone around World War I.

The landscape has healed its wounds quite cosmetically, as we shall see by choosing the left fork and keeping on Washington Street instead of rising with Route 127 and Langsford Street. Close on our left are what first appear to be twin ponds. Another look reveals water-filled quarry pits (map 3, 1), the preserve of the late sculptor Paul Manship, whose house and studio, as viewed from around the corner on Leverett Street, sit astride them. The easterly of the two pits is said to be eighty-five feet deep.

Lane's Cove

Washington Street is the old main road of Lanesville village, here a quiet avenue of timeworn and dignified clapboard houses. Cut granite is everywhere—foundations, walls, gateposts—though few homes are made of it from the ground up anywhere on Cape Ann. Too expensive.

Rejoining Langsford Street (laid out later, after the first quarries were opened), we take a sharp right and left down the grade by the sauna (Lanesville steamed with sauna in the days of the Finnish stonecutters' colony) and come out at Lane's Cove, the smallest harbor on the

9. *Lane's Cove was
dramatically created
by its breakwater.
The dory hauled up
on Flatstone Ledge
was as common here
as everywhere
around Cape Ann a
hundred years back.*

coast. It was created by a private company organized to build the break-water in the early 1830s, when Quincy men were blasting out the first commercial quarries on Cape Ann. The city bought out the company's rights to the cove in the 1960s and made a public landing of it, with a ramp, float, and parking.

Lane's Cove was as much a harbor for the shore fishermen as for the stone sloops and coasting schooners. Father unto son stowed trawl tubs, bait boxes, nets, floats, jigging lines, and lobster gear in a shantytown of fish shacks here and rowed or sailed wherry or dory, generally singlehanded, as far out as six or eight miles into the Bay for a day of fishing. Nor was it unusual for a man to labor back at dusk with a ton of codfish setting him down almost to his gunwales.

The flatstone ledge that first identified the cove makes a wading pool of it today. The heavy rusted rings and chains, and the cylindrical granite bollards for springlining the vessels to the piers, are still here, and vestiges of the derricks. Small boats have hauled up since colonial times at the end of the marsh where the stream meets the sea and the purple loosestrife grows.

Bay View: Plum and Hodgkins Coves

Following along Washington Street, we dip next into Plum Cove, a small and sheltered public beach, the only one on the Bay shore, with parking across the street. A public landing, too. Beach plums grew thick here once. So steep is the grade on each side of the cove that in the 1880s a trestle was erected to elevate the track across the bottom out of consideration for the horse cars.

10. *Looking east in the boom days of quarrying at Bay View. That's probably the Cape Ann Granite Company's railroad engine* Polyphemus *(named for the mythical giant Cyclops with a single eye) crossing Washington Street, the "Blue Church" in the distance.*

We move on above the sea.

That colorful and consummately political general of the Civil War, Benjamin F. Butler, bought up shore between Hodgkins and Diamond coves after he was relieved of his command at New Orleans in 1863 and camped on it with his sons in a tent during the summers of '63, '65, and '66, when he was elected to Congress from Gloucester's district, though a legal resident of Lowell, bragging that he campaigned "while I lived in a tent on the beach." In 1869 Congressman Butler interested his old comrade-in-arms, Colonel Jonas H. French, in organizing the Cape Ann Granite Company; granite, of course, was in great demand for public buildings authorized by Congress.

The friends built stone mansions on the slope above Hodgkins Cove—Butler's to the east—and he named their domain Bay View. The

11. Stone was literally the keystone of the heavy construction industry in 1886. The Cape Ann Granite Company's processing and loading works bordered Hodgkins Cove. Washington Street crosses the bridge and the railroad track at left; Davis Neck lies beyond.

company bought two hundred acres of land and used grout from the quarries it opened up to thrust out the long pier over the ledge on the north shore of the cove (originally "Hogskin," for reasons obscure) for its stonecutting sheds and railhead. There had been some crude quarrying back in the hills before Cape Ann Granite's arrival, some shore fishing out of the cove, and lumbering (the mill dam is still there on the stream site granted John Haraden by Gloucester in 1702); but it was Butler and French—a canny pair—who put Bay View on the map.

"The soil being cleared from a ledge and an examination having been made to see how the seams run," as a writer described the process at Bay View in 1879, "a steam drill is set to work boring two holes from ten to eighteen feet in depth and three inches in width, and two inches apart. A half keg of powder is put in these holes and ignited with electricity. The explosion lifts the ledge from seam to seam, usually in a straight line. Sometimes these lifts are 20,000 tons weight. The blasts do not smash the rock at all; a person is perfectly safe standing a few feet away.

"The section of the ledge thus broken off is split into smaller sections, to suit various purposes, with small hand drills and wedges. These pieces are taken to the yard by train, there to be worked into whatever shape desired, with hammer and chisel."

Possibly the largest stones ever blasted from Cape Ann were those used as the base sections of the equestrian statue of General Winfield Scott in Washington, which came from the company's Blood Ledge Quarry in 1873. The biggest weighed in at a hundred and fifty-one tons raw and snapped the rails on the track like a string of firecrackers as it rolled down to the cove. There it was refined to one hundred nineteen tons and swung aboard the three-masted schooner *Jonas H. French* with the rest of the base. The overburdened vessel was blown nine hundred miles off course and docked up in the Potomac several weeks late, having been given up for lost. Colonel French was so overjoyed at the safe arrival of his uninsured cargo, not to mention his namesake, that he sent Captain Harrington a gold watch.

Bay View was ruled by the Cape Ann Granite Company; it hired as many as six hundred men seasonally and owned tenements, a boardinghouse, and the grocery store. Years afterwards, the Consolidated Lobster Company took over the abandoned pier at Hodgkins Cove. At its zenith Consolidated circulated four million live lobsters annually through its seawater tanks in the former stone sheds and supplied the nation as broker for lobstermen from New England to Nova Scotia. Since 1971 Hodgkins Cove has been home to the marine biological research laboratory of the University of Massachusetts. There is a high-tide public landing and ramp here. Davis Neck, once two islands, parallels the pier across the cove. A watch house was built there nearly three hundred years ago to raise the alarm against French, Indians, and pirates, and in the last century the Massachusetts Humane Society maintained a life station, mainly to rescue mariners who were constantly running afoul of the always shifting sand bar at the entrance to the Annisquam River. Between the Neck and the pier Ben Butler moored his beloved schooner yacht *America*, first winner of the America's Cup, which he acquired from the Navy in a dubious deal in 1873.

The coastal ridge for half to three-quarters of a mile behind the Lanesville and Bay View shoreline is pitted with quarries, some big and filled with water, some piled with grout, some mere "motions," as the simple two-man surface operations producing paving stones were called. Quarry Street climbs up from Hodgkins Cove past the immense, fenced-in Klondike Quarry, a city reservoir now, and if we bear left over a tough road of jagged grout through the "Granny Pierce Pasture" we arrive at the dizzying brink of Nelson's and then Vernon's quarries (map 3, 2), both big and deep enough for high-diving exhibitions by the local kids.

Annisquam

Bay View halts at the door of the well-proportioned Village Church of 1830, which tends the only land entrance to Annisquam and, for some, its heavenly exit as well (map 3, 3). Squam is said to be Indian for a harbor in the mouth of a river. Once it was "Annis-Squam," perhaps a borrowing from Cape Ann. A squam is also a cheap yellow sou'wester hat that originated with the fishermen here. Anyway, the peninsular portion of Squam west of Lobster Cove, once called Planter's Neck, has been home to the white man since 1631.

The stance of its classic New England country church is a symbol of Squamism, for it was in rebellion against the distance to the meeting-house at the Green, now Grant Circle, that people here followed the example of the West Parishioners and in 1728 seceded from the First Parish and set themselves up as the Third Parish. Here at the head of Lobster Cove they built the antecedent to this church, handier to the scattered faithful around the top of the Cape from Goose Cove to Sandy Bay. The Third Parish was easily reached by water by way of two high-tide public landings, one just south of the church (marked now by a plaque), and another a few rods short of that on an unpaved way off Leonard Street. But even the Third Parish proved too far flung, and Sandy Bay in turn broke off as the Fifth in 1754 and set itself up as the town of Rockport in 1840. Squamism hung on, and indeed spread to Lanesville on one side and Riverdale on the other in 1879, when the three neighborhoods, chafing under Gloucester's achievement of cityhood six years earlier, talked darkly for a while about seceding as a separate town.

The vehicular route to Annisquam (drive slowly through these narrow streets) has relapsed to the roundabout forced on travelers for more than two hundred years. A bridge with a draw in it was built across

Lobster Cove in 1847 but closed in 1968. Rebuilt in 1989, it's restricted to foot travel, and Squam has resumed by fiat the special isolation it enjoyed in the prebridge days when it was a proud and self-reliant port that rivaled Gloucester Harbor. Even after the balance of fishing and commerce had tipped in favor of Gloucester, when Lobster Cove was too small and Squam Bar too shifty for vessels of large draft to enter, an 1856 atlas shows a dozen or more commercial wharves and two shipyards from Babson Point to the upper flats of Lobster Cove.

The cove is no longer dredged above the bridge, whose openings for the coasting schooners are a closed chapter. Leonard Street is sleepier, if possible, than ever. The peacefulness and the preservation of so many of the old houses along it, with their sociable lawns and gardens and rose arbors, would bring a smile to the benign features of "Father" Ezra Leonard, once pastor of the church—whose flock was so devoted that it followed him almost in a body when he abandoned the old orthodoxy for the new Universalism in 1811.

12. The Lobster Cove footbridge used to be open to vehicles—and opened to vessels such as the tall coasting schooner Lucy May of Cherryfield, Maine, warping through. Looking northeast around 1896.

Squam's Ipswich Bay shore was good for pasture and picnics and berrying and not much else until its subdivision into house lots. The roads of Rockholm and Norwood Heights are private, but we can thread through Norwood (George Norwood's pasture until 1895), being sure to keep a sight of the sea before us as a guide, and seek out the lighthouse on Wigwam Point, built in 1801 and rebuilt in 1897 (map 3, 4).

Squam Light, with its red warning sector to keep ships off the northwest shore, has a vestal purity about it, like a candle in the window. A picture book lighthouse. Off to the north and west the Bay is bluest of the blue on a cloudless day, a blue that deepens as the wind pipes up. Across the bar the dazzling dunes recede from Farm Point to the thin line of Plum Island dancing in the heat waves. The channel along the very edge of the long sandbar across the river's entrance from Squam is dredged so close aboard the ledge under the light that a spry thief with a long gaff could capture his dinner from the passing lobsterboat. Just over the rocks to the south, on this shining day of blues and browns and whites, Lighthouse Beach and the bathers could have been painted there from the palette of Prendergast.

Stray from the channel in your boat for but an instant, and you're aground on Squam Bar and courting embarrassment, if not disaster in a northeast storm. Generations ago an old man who knew whereof he spoke and also had little patience with believers in the Hereafter cut loose with this succinct verse:

> *Some people they call Christians how many things they tell*
> *About the land of Canaan where saints and angels dwell,*
> *But vessels built by human skill have never got so far*
> *But what they've got aground on Squam River Sandy Bar.*

A hundred and forty years ago, relates Charles Boardman Hawes in *Gloucester by Land and Sea*, the lightkeeper and his family occupied a one-room house here, kept a cow, ''and conducted their affairs with almost incredible simplicity. It is told of them that their kitchen gear consisted of a milkpan, an iron pot, and a dozen wooden spoons. They milked the cow into the pan, boiled hominy in the pot and poured it into the milk, and taking each one a wooden spoon, fell to with a will. Once when the minister was calling, one of the boys attempted to step across the pan and by fearful blunder put his bare foot squarely into the hominy and milk. Not a whit disturbed, the rest rapped him sharply on the leg with their spoons and continued eating as eagerly as before.''

On Leonard Street beyond Chester Square are Old Castle (1717), the Madam Goss place (1728), and then the village center (map 3, 5), namely: the old Village Hall, with library and auditorium, headquarters of the Village Hall Association; the venerable Leonard School, housing the Exchange and an art gallery; and sandwiched in behind the two, the Hose 8 Firehouse, home of the Historical Society. All but the library are summer operations. The peak of the season is the Annisquam Sea Fair.

From the middle of the footbridge at the bottom of Bridgewater Street it's hard to visualize schooners warping two hundred yards farther up the cove to Chard's Wharf, but they did. Down the cove, River Road must be sauntered to be appreciated. Rotary mowers clip the wharves now where once the berthed vessels poked their bowsprits overhead. The waterfront and anchorage are all yachts, with barely room for a workboat. Sailboat racing in Ipswich Bay has been keen since long before the Squam Dory Club formalized it in 1896, as keen as at Marblehead, and more relaxed. No liveried launchmen here.

13. *Annisquam Light and the boathouse of the Massachusetts Humane Society's lifesaving station, about 1870.*

A few paces beyond the weathered yacht club at River Road and Leonard Street are the houses of Captain Andrew Haraden and, diagonally across, Edward Haraden, both about 1700. Andrew had barely cleared Squam on a fishing trip in his new sloop *Squirrel* one April day in 1724 when he and his crew were taken by John Phillips and his pirate gang. Biding their time, Haraden and his men sprang upon their captors, turned the tables, and sailed *Squirrel* back to Squam, the disembodied visage of Phillips gazing gruesomely down from their masthead.

14. *From High Town, or Barberry Hill, across Lobster Cove in the early 1880s, Annisquam looked like Dogtown. To the left of Squam Rock on the ridge is D. A. Bulkley's "Crown Cottage," one of the village's first summer homes.*

Two hundred feet past Squam Rock Road on Walnut Street is the semipublic Squam Rock Land Trust reservation (map 3, 6). A short ascent to the pasture's edge brings you out on the rounded pate of ledge on which the glacier, with nice whimsy, deposited a smooth, sheer, enormous rock, like the apple on Master Tell's head, waiting for an arrow big enough to knock it off. "Young's Great Rock," as it used to be called, is insurmountable except by the most agile; but fortunately a smaller pebble close by gives a fine view of the Squam woods to the rear, the lighthouse through a dip in the trees ahead, and off to the left front the marshes and the Bay, punctuated by the comma of a sail, the dash of a motor cruiser's snowy wake.

No part of Gloucester is older than Annisquam, or more its own place. All its instincts are insular, fortified by the closing of the bridge to vehicles. And Squam is where a Squammer can return year after year to recapture the summer magic of a surely magical childhood. If there is about old Annisquam a certain self-satisfaction, it is well deserved.

Goose Cove

But Planter's Neck is not the whole of Squam. Look at Goose Cove on the map, its wings spread in awkward flight; run a line from the northeast wingtip to Diamond Cove, and you have created a head for Planter's Neck, the whole being a sort of turned-in cape bounded waterwise by the Bay, the River, and Goose Cove. Before the causeway, and Annisquam's bridge before that, provided shortcuts across the narrows, travelers to and from Squam had to swing clear inside of Goose Cove, which kept greater Annisquam even more to itself.

In those simple days Washington Street was merely a dead end lane from the Village Church, along the shaded slope of Barberry Hill above Lobster Cove, to Baker's farm in the triangle made by Goose Cove. The farmhouse in the field there, looking across from the causeway, is said to have been built in 1664 by Francis Norwood. It was acquired as a summer home in 1878 by Professor Alpheus Hyatt, a Boston zoologist and paleontologist, who made of it his Annisquam Seaside Laboratory. The location proved not entirely suitable, however, and within a year or two Hyatt joined in founding the Woods Hole marine biological laboratory as its first president. Thereby the Hyatt house and Annisquam can claim to be the birthplace of American oceanography.

An 1831 map shows a bridge across Goose Cove. The causeway was laid around 1834 and served as the dam for a tidal mill that operated here for about fifty years; the mill building is now restored as a private residence (map 3, 7). The Hodgkins family ran it and when they weren't grinding corn were sawing lumber. The waterwheel revolved horizontally. "On occasions when miller Hodgkins purchased corn," Harriet H. Mayor has recalled of the period around 1880, "a schooner thus laden would sail up the channel leading to Goose Cove, guided by a wooden channel post, long since sunk to rest, and lie along the north wall of the mill. The ship's bow lay so close to the road the bowsprit had to be telescoped to avoid blocking traffic. . . . If the ebb tide came in the night hours, the work of grinding must proceed, and I recall an eerie light, as from a single candle, burning in one of the mill windows while water churned from underneath the mill in dusky, glimmering streaks. The mill had the L that once held machinery for sawing up logs."

The Hodgkins mill put a much older one out of business, a gristmill conveniently located at that northeast end of Goose Cove where the old road from the Green to Squam and the Rockport road came together—the intersection today of Dennison, Bennett, and Holly streets (map 3, 8). The prettiest and shortest way to get there is along Dennison from the north end of the causeway. Most of the dam, the sluiceway, and the millpond are on private property. The house at the pond is believed to have been built in 1663 and for a long time was a tavern at this crossroads. On the south bank of the stream, across the road from the dam, is the small house once owned by "Marm" Killam; when it was rebuilt, deep channels were found in the floor where bags of corn by the ton had been dragged across.

Phantom Roads: Bennett Street and Saville Lane

A hundred yards east of the mill dam Bennett Street departs from Dennison up the hill and into the woods, headed for Lobster Cove. Leaving the first few houses behind, it fades to a woodland path of apparent antiquity that skirts a deep, wooded ravine and passes the small Jordan and Gore quarries, almost hidden from sight in the right-hand brush, all tumbled and askew with grout, mottled with lichen, and over a hundred years old. Bennett Street, no street at all, comes out

15. *Formerly known as the "Customs House" for the contraband concealed therein by slightly errant fishermen, Wheeler's fishhouse and wharf in the 1890s was on the Lobster Cove shore just short of today's Annisquam Market at the curve beyond. Across the water, Bennett Street heads over Barberry Hill for Goose Cove.*

on the highway above Lobster Cove and below the summer home of
the late playwright Russel Crouse.

A long time ago Sandy Bay fishermen caught in an easterly gale on
Ipswich Bay would run for shelter in Squam River, anchoring probably in Lobster Cove and rowing the dory up to the public landing at
the east end of Goose Cove. They'd haul up here and hike the two
and a half miles over Dennison Street and the Dogtown moors to home.

Dennison Street today peters out to a Dogtown path, but there is
a short side tramp well worth the taking for the curious (beware the
mosquitoes) in search of the "Frenchman's cellar" and Jesse Saville's
tanpit.

We bear right around the millpond up Dennison and turn into the
woods between the first pair of stone gateposts. The trail follows a steep
ravine above a brook and passes through a good stand of hardwoods
and a dramatic grove of fine tall hemlock—said to be the only such
east of Squam River.

Here in this deep, mysterious, twisting gully, long-forgotten stone
walls are so indistinguishable from the chaotic terminal moraine left
by the glacier on the slopes that they seem piled up merely to remind:
"These are my rocks over here; yours are yonder."

Our path crosses the stream over a mossy culvert of granite shafts;
fifty feet off to the right, on a wooded knoll, are the remains of "Frenchman's cellar" in local lore (map 3, 9)—French, because if we strike off
through the woods about due north, another fifty feet to the next knoll,
we find another boulder on which are crudely carved a *fleur-de-lis* and,
beneath that:

L. LEMAY

APR. 17

1881

L. Lemay may not have had anything to do with the remnant of
a cellar. More likely, the path we've been following is pretty clearly
an extension of a paper road, Saville Lane, and we may have stum-
bled upon the home site of Jesse Saville, who operated a pit for the
tanning of animal hides near his farm. To find this tanpit (map 3, 10),
we pursue our path as it melts into Saville Lane in the shadow of a
huge overhanging ledge. Here, at the bottom of the most gothic

16. A serene sentinel, the Annisquam Village Church and the public landing up in Lobster Cove were caught on an 8 x 10 glass-plate negative by Martha Rogers around 1900.

ravine on Cape Ann, is the swamp where Saville and his sweating men dug out a broad bog and strung hides to soak in a solution of tanbark stripped from the oak and mayhap the ancestors of those unique hemlocks we passed.

Saville achieved immortality of sorts in his capacity as the king's customs officer charged with trying to stop the smuggling of his fellow Gloucestermen. An enraged gang of them disguised as black men and Indians came here on the night of March 23, 1770, hauled Saville out of bed, dragged him into town, and tanned his own hide with tar before they set him loose to find his way back home through the woods to Squam.

We gain the ridge that ghostly Saville Lane follows to ghostly Bennett Street in the footsteps of that Gloucester tanning party, go left and come out to the sunlight of Dennison Street and the blue water of Goose Cove (if the tide is in), leaving Annisquam—and history for a moment—behind.

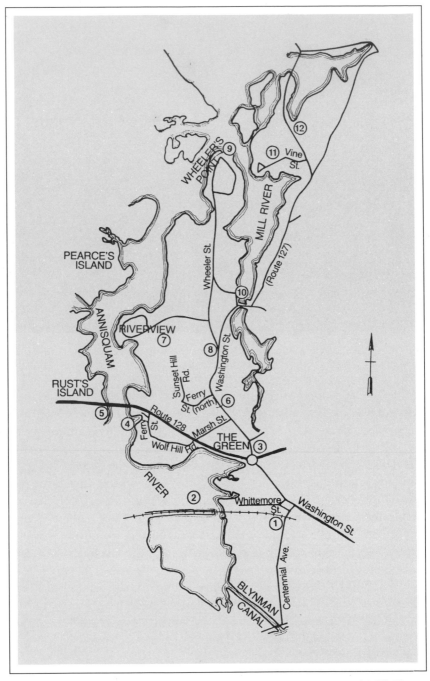

Map 4. Annisquam and Mill Rivers

ANNISQUAM
AND MILL RIVERS

The Cut to Goose Cove

Blynman Canal

There is an excitement about the Cut, which is what we call Blynman Canal. Go there day or night, any season—when an easterly slashes rain across and whips up spray from the surf smashing on the seawall, or when the June sun sparkles on the harbor and they cast the blossoms on the ebb for the souls of the men who went down to the sea and did not return, or in the fullness of the evening when the rising moon profiles Eastern Point and sheds diamonds on the water.

The red lights flash on, the siren screams, the gates swing across the boulevard, the gears grind, and the jaws of the drawbridge crack open to let a fishing dragger through. For a few minutes Gloucester is almost an island. Then the jaws descend and shut with a toothsome click, the gates swing clear, and the line of summer traffic drones across again, always with that urgency: can we make it before the next one shuts us off?

Especially before Route 128 spanned the river in 1953, the Cut bridge has symbolized Gloucester's isolation and contrariness. Since 1907, when the state dredged the channel and rebuilt and electrified the bridge, the machinery has waited, as if it had a life of its own, to get stuck half way up or down on sunny summer Sunday afternoons, each time requiring a citywide search for Sylvester Deering, the only electrician in town who talked its language. Before that, back to just after the Civil War, when the canal was reopened, the bridge was cranked or swung by hand, and some local magician with a different bag of tricks had to conjure with it.

46

17. *Blynman Bridge (looking toward the harbor) in 1900 swung upriver on a hand-cranked turntable at left. The ledge beneath, not yet blasted out, made the Cut unnavigable at low water.*

18. *These "sand hogs" are digging the tunnel under Blynman Canal for the water main from the new West Gloucester reservoirs, probably in 1884. Hey, who invited that rat to the party?*

In 1643 the town gave Pastor Blynman permission to cut a ditch through the isthmus between the Annisquam River and the harbor and to build the first swinging bridge over it. Blynman's "cut" could save a hard outside ocean passage around Cape Ann to Squam or the eastward, or could float wood to the harbor from the western hills, and skippers paid him toll, willingly or not. However, a storm filled his cut with sand in 1704; it was cleared, only to fill again in 1723.

It was another hundred years before the Blynman Canal was reopened in 1823, with a drawbridge whose backers had high hopes for steam. But the river turned out to be too narrow for steamboats and too hazardous for all but the smallest craft to sail. Moreover, the Eastern Railroad insisted on a fixed bridge upriver for its new Gloucester branch from Salem in 1847. Consequently, in 1848 the canal was filled with a solid east-west roadway. Not for twenty more years was all at last resolved when for the fourth time the Cut was opened and bulkheaded, and another bridge built, all for the purpose of passing boatloads of granite through from a new quarry on Wolf Hill. Reasoning that what couldn't flow over could run under, the Gloucester Water Supply Company a hundred years ago built the big brick tunnel under the Cut that carries the mains from Bond Hill reservoir and other utilities to town.

So for a hundred and twenty years of its three hundred and fifty, Blynman Canal has been no canal at all.

The most rewarding exploration of Squam River is of course by small boat—oaring a skiff or learning to sail, as this writer did fifty-five years ago—for right down on the water is the intimacy of the tide, which is either for you or against you, and the nearness of marsh and sandbar and shore on all sides.

Bridge Street Burying Ground

But the land view has the merit of overview, so let's climb Centennial Avenue through the old harbor pasture. A few feet south of the narrow bridge that vaults the tracks (stubbornly called by people "Blue Bridge" long after the color had been changed), behind the granite posts and iron gate on the left, is Gloucester's oldest cemetery, the Bridge Street Burying Ground (map 4, 1). (This end of Centennial was Bridge Street a hundred and twenty years ago, and Burying Ground Lane before that.)

Mingled here with the earth and the broken bottles on this playground of generations of neighborhood children are the dust of the settlers and the bones of the first families of colonial Cape Ann: Babson, Parsons, Somes, Ellery, Riggs, Allen, Plummer, Rogers, Low, and others unmarked because the markers have been smashed.

A stone that has escaped destruction memorializes one of the Minute Men of Gloucester whom we have already met: "BE IT REMEMBERED THAT HERE LIES THE BODY OF THE HONBLE PETER COFFIN ESQR WHO DIED FEBRY 14TH 1796 AGED 72 YEARS. HE WAS A TRUE PATRIOT, A PACIFIC MAGISTRATE, AN EXAMPLAREY CHRISTIAN AND A FRIEND TO MANKIND."

Efforts are being made by Gloucester people appreciative of their heritage to tidy up and protect this hallowed ground with the help of state funds.

Done Fudgin'

Just across the Blue Bridge, to the left on the height of Curtis Square, is Meetinghouse Hill, on which the settlers are believed to have built their first crude place of worship in the 1630s. Descend Whittemore Street, and we come to the bend in the river behind the stilled Cape Ann Anchor Works (destined for housing) on the north side of the railroad drawbridge, known as Done Fudgin' (map 4, 2).

Historian Babson says that when timber was being floated from West Parish through the Cut to the harbor two hundred and seventy years ago, Done Fudgin' was where the men were finished "fudging" their rafts or boats—poling them, or perhaps simply making hard work of it, which is another meaning—because it is here where the incoming tides from either end of the river meet, and where they part on the ebb. Hence, if they had been working against the current as they approached Done Fudgin', the boatmen could rest from here on and let the fair tide do their work.

In recent years people have called the stretch of river at the public landing and ramp off Centennial Avenue behind the High School, where the city "poor farm" used to be, Done Fudgin'. But it must in reality be here beyond the railroad bridge. Compare the view with Fitz Hugh Lane's *Looking Up Squam River from Done Fudging* of the 1850s, at the Cape Ann Historical museum. They are the same.

The railroad bridge wasn't made to open until 1872, when a swing draw was installed. The late Edward H. Lane related that when it was a fixed span on trestles, boys caught crossing in midspan by a train coming would flatten themselves between the rails while it roared over them. During the first severe winters after the Gloucester branch came through in 1847, the salt ice built up ten feet thick beneath this first bridge. On several occasions a high tide lifted this floe up under the bridge and sucked the piles clean out of the mud. This made such an arch of it that the train could hardly manage the grade. Finally the ice lifted the bridge so high that only the locomotive was able to cross, leaving the cars at the West Gloucester station, and the passengers to travel back and forth to town in hacks. At last the piles were cut off, and the span was narrowed with solid fill. So said Mr. Lane.

Meetinghouse Green

When Pastor Blynman and his flock of dissidents arrived from the Plymouth Colony about 1641, still having nonfishing pursuits in mind, they fixed upon the lush meadow between the head of Mill River and an inlet of the Annisquam—Meetinghouse Plain, or Green, which didn't entirely escape the extension of Route 128 across the Squam River three hundred and eleven years later.

A study in contrasts. Grant Circle and its shopping area have all but obliterated the head of the Squam River marsh and the public landing, where in times past small boats could pull in to within thirty yards of Washington Street. Not much more than a hundred years ago this earliest of Gloucester roads still swirled up in dust under the hooves and wheels of the stagecoach to Squam. The tracks for the horse cars were laid in 1886, late coming, for within ten years they gave way to the electric trolleys, whose powerhouse was an anomalous landmark here on the edge of the tide. And then the auto, and now, since 1953, the not so merry merry-go-round of the traffic circle.

On the west side of Washington Street beyond and above the circle is the Green, split by Ashland Place. In the shade of the tall trees a boulder plaque marks the "Plain" where four successive houses of worship were built, the first soon after the town's incorporation in 1642, the last standing here until 1840.

Across Washington Street are two venerable monuments to the carpenter's art (map 4, 3). The Babson-Alling house on the right has been here since about 1740, renowned affectionately for its solid yet graceful colonial construction and its country gardens. The mysterious pens in the attic eaves were said by the owners to have hidden slaves escaping via the Underground Railroad. Yet slavery was an accepted part of colonial Gloucester; we may hope our predecessors provided better quarters than this.

The White-Ellery house next door, though built probably before 1650, has been here since 1953. For three hundred years it stood on the Green south of the meetinghouse, facing the marshes. The Cape Ann Historical Association acquired it in 1947. In 1953 the "Histori-

19. *The horsecar cuts across what is now the east side of Grant Circle as it rattles north on Washington Street at Meetinghouse Green about 1889. Directly beyond is the White-Ellery house on its original site, the Babson-Alling house on the right, as always.*

cal" raised the funds to move it to its present site to make way for the northside lanes of Grant Circle. During restoration, they concluded that the White-Ellery House was not built in 1703 for the First Parish's third pastor, John White, as had been believed, but a half-century earlier, making it one of the oldest in America. James Stevens kept it as a tavern and sold it in 1740 to Captain William Ellery, who did likewise, and it remained in the Ellery family until the Historical bought it.

By a turn of fate, the extension of Route 128 restored the Green to its former position as the crossroads of Gloucester after two centuries of slumber following the shift of the town center to the harbor. In those unhurried days the backwaters of Mill and Annisquam rivers were a mere two hundred and fifty yards apart here, and this made the "Neck of House Lots," as the settlers called the peninsula between the two, almost a landlocked island.

Hence it is that a few old-timers still refer to this site of the original settlement as "up in town."

Wolf and Ferry Hills

Marsh Street leaves Washington on the left for Wolf and Ferry hills. Wolves in Gloucester? Well, in 1754 the town posted a bounty of four pounds for killing a grown one and half that for a cub. They must have been around, howling in the woods, presumably, of Wolf Hill. The ledge out here is a pleasant pink, and the company that opened the quarry after the Civil War thought it had a good thing. But the rock was too soft for building, and they went out of business, leaving behind two legacies: the reopened Cut, and their road, which brought to Wolf Hill its first summer cottagers.

Bearing right under the Route 128 overpass on Wolf Hill Road, we pick up Ferry Street to Trynall Cove, another high-tide public landing of antiquity with limited parking (map 4, 4). The Hodgkinses shuttled their West Parish ferry between here and Biskie Head, right across the river on Rust's Island (map 4, 5). An early mapmaker spelled the cove's name "Trenel," probably a corruption of treenail, pronounced "trunnel," a wooden ship fastening, preferably of locust; there may have been a grove of them here.

The Addison Gilbert Hospital (map 4, 6) was built in 1897 with a $100,000 legacy from its namesake, a public-spirited Gloucester businessman, on Jonathan Brown's thirteen-acre farm. The nurses first lived in the old farmhouse. Today's modern facility serves all of Cape Ann.

First left beyond the hospital, Ferry Street ends in a dirt road down to the right (having been cut off from Wolf Hill by the Route 128 bridge embankment). The dirt road deposits the boat lover at the Squam River yard founded in 1907 by Nicholas (Monty) Montgomery and operated continuously since then by son Herb and now by grandson Dave, all master boatwrights.

Riverview, Sunset Rock, and The Poles

Across from the Babson farm, whose cows not so many years ago supplied Gloucester with milk from the Riverdale meadows, Wheeler Street climbs to the left off Washington under the brow of The Poles, or Poles Hill, which may be how the natives mouthed the name of one Powel, who settled around here. The first left runs to Riverview, the most westerly point on the Neck of House Lots.

When the writer was a boy at the family summer cottage in Riverview, this lane separated a truck farm on the right from a good blueberrying pasture on the left, which we climbed, avoiding the cows and cow flops, for the reward of a spectacular view from Sunset Rock. That view today is as grand as ever.

To get there we return to Ferry Street (north), take the first right on Sunset Hill Road to the roadblock where Periwinkle Lane goes left. Up the gravel road, Sunset Rock (map 4, 7) rises unmistakably on our left front, the granite hump of The Poles (map 4, 8) on our right. Any of various narrow footpaths through the low-bush blueberries and huckleberries (or whortleberries—it was once called Whortleberry Hill) lead to the bare and breezy summit and a three hundred and sixty-degree panorama of Gloucester: the West Gloucester hills, the Route 128 bridge, Little River, Squam River, Rust's and Merchant's islands, Jones Creek, West Parish, Ipswich Bay, the dunes, the mountains of New Hampshire and Maine, Squam Light, Dogtown, the city, the harbor, and the Breakwater.

Most any path leading east of Sunset Rock will twist its way around the berry bushes and the brier and the sweet pepper, through a dip and by a patch of bog, to the stony crown of The Poles. Here's another prospect of the Bay, and a dizzying one of the length of Mill River, Riverdale, the O'Maley School, downtown, the harbor, and Washington Street's rooftops at our feet.

A short distance beyond Riverview Road, Apple Street leads to Corliss Landing, a high-tide public landing with a ramp to Annisquam River and parking.

The Islands

The pioneer summer camper on Squam River was probably George W. Smith of Boston, who put Shiloh Lodge on Rust's Island in the 1850s. He was soon followed by other discoverers of the river's delights such as the Boston Boat Club. Storer Crafts of Boston bought half of Rust's Island around 1908, intending to build a hotel, but his plan fell through.

Simeon Merchant kept livestock on Pearce's Island and in 1869 built summer cottages for rent. The first campers, mostly Gloucester people like newspaper publisher and editor George Procter, roughed it on what they began calling Merchant's Island. Procter would take the Squam stagecoach from his downtown newspaper office after work, walk the road to Brown's Landing at Riverview (then Rocky Point), and row his dory across the river to the island and the welcoming shouts of his children. On a moonlit evening they might oar up Jones

20. *Summer innocence, about 1874, on the Annisquam River from "Maiden's Retreat Bluff," Merchant's Island.*

Creek and bob for eels, as "Uncle Sim" Merchant taught them, off the long stone pier. There were plenty of lobsters to be caught in the creek then, and folks could dig a basket of clams from the flats at low tide in no time at all.

It's said that before the channel was dredged in 1910 you could walk at low tide from West Landing, the public landing at the end of the grass path off Thurston Road on Thurston's Point, over stepping stones across Squam River to the sandbar and thence to Merchant's (Pearce's) Island.

Wheeler's Point

When Pearce owned it, it was Pearce's Point, then Stanwood's, then Gee's (hard *g*) before a Wheeler bought it some time before 1830; the thrust of settlement had long since shifted from the Neck of House Lots to Gloucester Harbor, and Wheeler Street remained a country lane, resisting even reconstruction by the summer people after the Civil War. At the end of the road on the left is the oldest house on the Point, the Wheeler House in fact (map 4, 9). A timeworn saltbox with a lordly view of the river, it's believed to have been built around 1650 by Richard Dyke, and it has a story. At the river's edge is what's left of a stone and log wharf that may be where Captain Gee carried on his fishing business in Revolutionary times.

The story goes back to June 13, 1814. We were at war with England again, and Lieutenant Henry Edward Napier, commanding the British frigate *Nymphe* standing off Squam, had sent in two barges of men to set fire to the sloop *Diligence* off Gee's Point, with a warning to the people here that if they tried to save her he'd cannonade the only house on the Point, namely this one, then owned by William Pearce. Being good Gloucestermen, the residents ignored the threat, and Napier was as good as his word. He fired off his twelve-pounder with effect. Since that day, owner after owner of this house has passed on the cannonball, though the hole has been patched. Years ago the old place was a tea room.

Down on the left above a backwash of Squam River, before you get to the Wheeler House, is the oldest continually operating boatyard on Cape Ann, where George Wheeler was building workboats and yachts as early as the 1870s.

21. *The tidal gristmill at Riverdale about 1900 is still operating. Storehouse is at left, sluiceway visible under the dam at right, electric trolley wire over the tracks.*

Riverdale

We leave the Neck of House Lots by the left fork on Wesley Street, pass the Wesleyan Cemetery, and are back on Washington Street. Here it crosses Mill River into Riverdale over the tidal dam whose foundation stones were laid across the creek some time soon after 1652 (map 4, 10).

This was Riverdale Mills.

To build a new society in a new world the pioneers must first have shelter against the winter and food to carry them through it; that meant wood and corn, and mills to saw and grind. They watched the tide surge up this creek from the Annisquam River twice a day, and Alewife Brook pour in from the head of it up at the Green, and somebody got an idea.

The brook's wine-colored water (from the rust of bog iron in Brier Swamp) already was turning the wheels of two small mills upstream when these ingenious millers dammed across the flats and made a tidal millpond here. The location couldn't have been better—less than a mile from the Green; astride the crossroads between Squam, the Neck of House Lots, and Sandy Bay; easily reached by water; possessed of a supply of power as long as the moon stayed up—power enough, in fact, for two.

The first was a sawmill built at the western end of the dam (hence the early name Sawmill Dam) not long after 1652. Then in 1677 the town gave Pastor John Emerson license to repair it and cut up to 20,000 feet of boards a year, and to erect a corn mill alongside. As it had in giving Pastor Blynman the privilege of digging his Cut and collecting tolls, this was the town's way of supporting in part, at least, its ministers in the times before the First Amendment to the Constitution.

Mr. Emerson ran both mills until his death in 1700. The properties and rights passed through several hands, and by the Revolution the sawmill was out of commission, apparently forever. Stephen and Edward Brown, father and son, owned the corn mill from 1835, and Levi Brackett ran it for them until 1875, when Albert Dodge became the owner. The stones ground slowly to a halt some time before World War I, and the buildings were torn down in 1925.

Thus for some two hundred and sixty years the sawmill or the corn mill or both were in practically continuous operation here at this crossroads of the settlers on Mill River, yet few today remember even how they looked. Lyman F. Allen earned pocket money in this vestige of the seventeenth century as a boy of eight in 1904 and told the writer how he shoveled corn from the wagons that carried it from the freight cars at the Depot into the mill's conveyer, which moved by water power via belts. Miller Rufus Simpson paid him ten cents for emptying a two- or three-ton wagonload.

The larger building was for storage. The machinery was in the smaller. When the tide was at the flood and filled the pond, the gates closed automatically against the ebb and held the head back until half tide, when the fall was sufficient to keep the wheel on the go. Grinding continued until the next half tide on the flow, which amounted to around twelve hours of it, day and night when the job warranted. The waterwheel rotated horizontally. The granite stones were eighteen to twenty-four inches thick to start with and wore down so fast that fresh grooves had to be cut in them periodically to keep the ground corn spewing out properly. One of the stones stands on end outside the store at the site today. The conveyer that was fed corn by Lyme Allen funneled the grain between the stones, while another conveyer caught the flour, meal, or cracked corn (depending on the grind) and trundled it off into hundred-pound bags. Before teams brought the corn from the Depot, Allen was pretty sure, it came to the mill on the flood tide in flat-bottomed sloops. Beside the monument is a high-tide public landing and ramp.

In the cool bowels of the mill the boys of Riverdale knew where to look in one eddy for the fat smelt, in another hiding place for the wily eels, and in a third for the alewives. Way up the creek and in the brook where they swam to spawn, alewives made a fishery worth pursuing one hundred seventy years ago, and the owner of Sawmill Dam was required by the town to open his gate and let them upriver to spawn each year. Darn few alewives make it now; the floodgates have been locked shut, the millpond is full of fresh water, and the environment was torn apart and drastically rearranged for the O'Maley School, which besides educating Gloucester's middle-grade children is the scene every March of the city's immensely popular Folklife Festival.

We leave Sawmill Dam to today's youngsters and climb Washington Street above Mill River's east bank. The creek has been good to Riverdale—sawing its wood, grinding its corn, bringing fish to its doorsteps, and providing clams for steaming and baiting with such generosity that a writer of the 1890s, finding the shore cluttered with clamdiggers' shacks and white with piles of shells, exclaimed that "most of the houses in the village have been paid for out of discounts from the clam banks."

The trolley car motormen in 1892, two years after the electrification of the horse cars, found the streets of Riverdale likewise cluttered—

with cows wandering from Dogtown pasture down onto the tracks, much to their irritation, especially after dark. There'd been some collisions. Would folks please keep their cows fenced?

At The Willows the first road to Squam (now Holly Street) struck off through the woods around Goose Cove before the causeway was built, but we bear around the curve and take Vine Street on the left for a quick exploration of Riggs Point.

Riggs Point Road (left fork) comes close enough to the shore in a couple of places to give a fine sweep of Mill River clear to Riverdale Mills. On the crest of the field above us sits the Riggs homestead commanding point and river. This low, tawny-shingled, gambrel-roofed relic is attributed to Thomas Riggs in 1660 (map 4, 11). Riggs was one of the few settlers to whom writing came easily, so they made him their first schoolmaster, named him town clerk for fifty one years, elected him a selectman for twenty, and sent him to the Great and General Court in Boston in 1700. Tom Riggs was one of the five courageous selectmen of Gloucester who stood trial up in Salem and was fined for refusing to pay taxes levied in 1688 by the arbitrary Governor Andros and his Council without the consent of the taxed—an issue on which more would be heard.

Like Gee's Point across the narrows, this was a good sheltered fishing station and handy to Ipswich Bay, and Riggs's descendants were in the business here for many years.

Along the last of Riverdale before Goose Cove, young willows are taking hold of the roadside where the giants until a few years ago blended their branches overhead to form a green arcade for the traveler. The original Annisquam (actually Riverdale) Willows were planted to reinforce the road with their roots when it was being built up through the marsh here. The gravel road up to the right before the causeway leads to the parking area of the Goose Cove Reservation of the Essex County Greenbelt Association (map 4, 12). You can circumnavigate the reservation by a shoreside walking path. This tract of twenty-six acres on the southeast slope above the cove was rescued from housing development by a group of Annisquam residents who bought it and gave it to Greenbelt. In so doing, they preserved a hillside that in spring drifts to the shore amidst clouds of fragrant shadbush bloom.

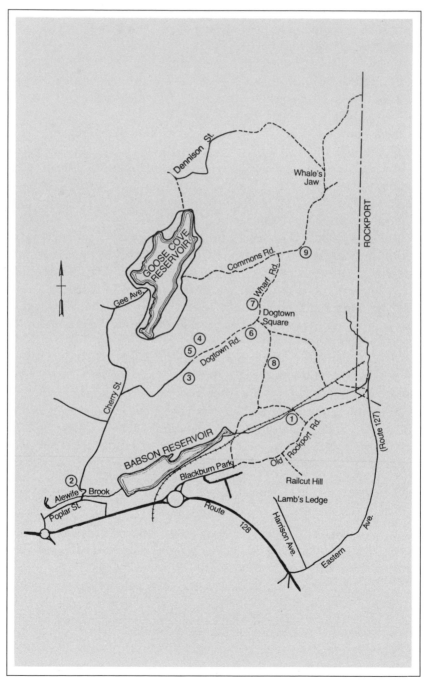

Map 5. Dogtown

CHAPTER 5

DOGTOWN

D ogtown is where you go when you have to get away, there or out on the water. It is the lonely highland of Cape Ann, empty of habitation, abandoned by the dogs and even by the cows that used to find thin pasture there, left to the ghosts of its deserted village. It's where you're off to with your blueberry bucket, or for a hike, when the world is too much with you.

A few hours up Dogtown stumbling over the stony paths, swatting mosquitoes, hearing the winds rattle the dry brush, pondering the pitiful cellar holes, wondering how anyone could have lived in such a spooky place, are enough to restore sociability.

Dogtown's peculiar therapeutic qualities were well grasped by one of its old-time denizens, Aunt Rachel Smith. Every spring fever time she would mix her mystic concoction of foxberry leaves, spruce tops, and such greeneries and would descend into town to peddle this brew from door to door. "Now ducky," Aunt Smith would cackle to the lady of the house, "I've come down to bring a dire drink, for I know you feel springish."

The power of Dogtown was also sensed by Roger W. Babson, Gloucester's renowned seer of the business cycle. Babson took advantage of the special psychological susceptibility of escapees to the place to buck them up with one-liners carved on the boulders at unexpected turns in the way, such as: GET A JOB; IF WORK STOPS, VALUES DECLINE; and the most heartwringing of all: HELP MOTHER.

By far the greater part of this uninhabited midland of over five square miles is in Gloucester, absolutely bedeviled with grown-over pasture, rocks, and swamps stagnating in pockets of the ledge. "This being the last place created," goes an old saying, "all the rocks not needed in the rest of the earth were dumped here."

What on earth, then, induced some sixty or so families to build homes up here on the parallelogram of moor that extends about a mile east of Riverdale village, called by this odd name of Dogtown?

Its foremost student, the late Charles E. Mann, believed that the entire area was as empty of human life as it is today until 1719, when a distribution of the town's open land made lots here available to every male over twenty-one, many the sons of settlers. A map of 1741 shows that twenty-five families, among them some of Gloucester's leading, had moved up. Mann suggests simple reasons: population explosion and proximity to the center of town, which was then the Green.

After the Revolution the revival of fishing and Gloucester's entry into foreign commerce quickened the shift of people toward the harbor. The houses of Dogtown not retained by widows of men missing in the war passed into the hands of the poorest class. Dogtown declined into rural slumdom, way up back out of sight and sound, peopled by a dwindling band of half-starved characters romanticized by poets and writers of a later generation as rustic curiosities. The last of them was taken off to the poorhouse in 1830.

Chroniclers and historians preferred to overlook Gloucester's ghetto, and by the time Mann took it up, no one was left to tell the tale. The name has been commonly attributed to the dogs supposedly kept by the poor women to protect themselves against pirates and ruffians while their men were off to the Revolution.

Perhaps we need look no farther than to "a heath" said to be about five or six miles from the Merrimack River on the outskirts of Newbury, where there existed a "Dog-Town" around the time of the Revolution strikingly similar to Gloucester's. This other Dogtown was described by Samuel L. Knapp in his 1838 life of the eccentric self-styled "Lord" Timothy Dexter of Newburyport, an account considerably antedating our Historian Babson's. Knapp's satirical yet sympathetic tale of these impoverished but proud "Dog-Towners" to the north fits their miserable counterparts on Cape Ann to a T, even to their reliance on the sale to the neighboring gentry of slightly alcoholic herbal concoctions in the manner of Aunt Rachel Smith.

So much for mystery. Today we're concerned with preserving our Dogtown's 3,600 acres as a great park, as a vital watershed, and as a wildlife sanctuary. About six hundred acres are still privately owned.

Four hundred more are publicly owned in Rockport. The city of Gloucester worked its way through a labyrinth of land titles to acquire another eight hundred or more in the spirit of Roger Babson, who gave 1,150 acres of the Alewife Brook watershed to the people of Gloucester for a public reservoir and reservation in memory of his father and grandfather, both of whom had roamed and loved Dogtown as he did. In 1930 the city dammed the brook at the end of Poplar Street and created Babson Reservoir, the first east of Squam River to supplement the supply that hitherto flowed wholly from West Parish through the single tired old main in the tunnel under the Cut.

The Dogtown Advisory Committee appointed by then Mayor Richard Silva in 1985 has made material strides in cleaning up and cleaning out the area, banning vehicles, and making it quite safe once again for public enjoyment.

The Old Rockport Road

So let's begin the Dogtown ramble on the south watershed of the Babson Reservoir, which was created by the newest dam on Alewife Brook, with a search for the oldest on Cape Ann.

First we must find the original main road that the settlers laid out from Meetinghouse Green to Sandy Bay. It followed the present Poplar Street, turned right on Maplewood Avenue, left on Gloucester Avenue (which two centuries later leapt over the railroad gorge on its well-known mortarless stone bridge), and then continued roughly parallel with Alewife Brook, joining Eastern Avenue a tenth of a mile beyond the Rockport line. This Old Rockport Road was little used after the harbor became the center of town, making Eastern Avenue the more direct route; but for a short period it was important because it led to the site of the first harnessing of water power in behalf of the permanent settlement of 1642.

When Route 128 was extended to Eastern Avenue in 1953, Blackburn Circle obliterated a section of the Old Rockport Road. We pick it up again on foot at the end of the access road to the Blackburn Industrial Park, just below the Varian plant. Before pushing along, the curious may want to climb to the top of Railcut (earlier Lookout) Hill, at two hundred and five feet the highest in Gloucester east of the river, just to say they've been there. Strike off up and over the terminal moraine on your right and find the old woods road that brings you to the remains of the brick chimney at the summit, where the overgrowth blocks what was described in 1896 as "a magnificent ocean view...one of the grandest outlooks which is afforded in Gloucester's fair borders." Some selective clearing would open up the world.

Between stone walls of antiquity, Old Rockport Road skirts an impressive stream of stones, the terminal moraine dumped by the melting glacier on the lower slope of Railcut Hill on our right, and after a quarter of a mile or so brings us by a clearing on the left. This leads down a dry washout to a glade of great trees and the gurgling waters of Alewife Brook, deep brown from the iron ore in the swamp upstream. So this is why they called it Wine Brook. Extending across, between a huge boulder and the railroad track, is the still well-defined hump of the colonists' first dam (map 5, 1). The city breached it in 1932 in order to drain the millpond the dam had held back for two hundred eighty years. The brook was more of a torrent before its main source at Cape Pond was cut off for the Rockport water supply, and the fall of the dam ranged up to fifteen feet. Through most of the year the settlers hauled in timber for sawing into lumber, suspending that operation at harvest time to grind corn.

This first industrial operation on the Cape was apparently made obsolete after a few years by the more efficient and central tidal mill at Riverdale. The location has much natural beauty and of course historical interest, marred only by the presence of occasional burned and abandoned vehicles.

The deepest terminal moraine around was called Lamb's Ledge in the old days when sheep grazing on the southern edge of Dogtown grazed too close and fell in or got trapped between the boulders. Indeed, so close are the rocks almost everywhere on Dogtown that the sheep's noses had to be tapered on a grindstone so that they could get at the grass between them, according to an authoritative family source. Some remnants of Lamb's Ledge can be seen between the dead end of Harrison Avenue, off Eastern Avenue, and the industrial park fill that has all but obliterated this remarkable natural feature.

Alewife, or Wine, Brook swells mightily into Babson Reservoir behind the dam at the end of Poplar Street, then dribbles out from under on its old course toward the Riverdale millpond. A couple of years after the men built that first mill dam on Cape Ann off Old Rockport

Road, the General Court in Boston gave Gloucester twenty pounds out of a gift the colony had received from Richard Andrews, "a godly man of London," towards erecting another mill. This Gloucester did across Alewife Brook, right about at the west entrance bridge to Poplar Park, the elderly housing development.

Pastor John Emerson ground the town's meal here for a few years before he took over the tide mill at Riverdale in 1677. The dam is about gone.

Beyond the cemetery near the Maplewood Avenue junction was a spring that joined the brook, known as "The Iron Dipper" for what hung there on a chain for the use of the thirsty.

Up Cherry Street

Cherry Street crosses the brook over an interesting granite culvert of great age, makes a sharp and dangerous S-curve around and over Fox Hill (map 5, 2), and continues on along the western slope of Dogtown. This was a hard climb for a team of horses or a yoke of oxen and remains so for a loaded truck today. When Dogtown was on the downhill grade but still inhabited, two extortionary Dogtowners maintained an ambush on the inside curve.

The senior, as Charles Mann relates, was Lucy George. Luce was lank and lath-legged, and professed to be a witch. She'd so hex the oxen at the brook they'd not look at Fox Hill until the driver paid her tribute in corn—or she'd jinx a load of wood so it wouldn't stay on the wagon until she'd had her pick.

Luce's understudy was her niece Thomasine Younger, short and dumpy, who substituted invective for the black art. When she heard a clatter on the bridge below, Tammy would throw open her window and call for a mackerel or a sample of whatever else happened to be going by. Most drivers preferred to toss her something to the torrent of abuse if they didn't.

Dogtown Road

Off Cherry Street a quarter of a mile beyond Reynard Street, unmarked Dogtown Road runs up to the right. The bad blacktop degenerates to the worse as we bounce by a freshwater spring down to the left and park in the clearing by the gravel pit (map 5, 3), making sure to lock and leave nothing valuable behind. We're about to enter the most ghostulated section of Dogtown.

A word of caution. The walks described here will stick to the more familiar beaten paths of this deserted village. Yet there are miles of old roads on the Common, confused paths and turnoffs that lead no- where. Distances are farther than they look on the map, and some of the boulders that Roger Babson had carved with identifying cellar num- bers are obscured by brush. The road in some places is rocky and tough on the feet, in others slick with mud and puddles. One wrong turn can befuddle the most experienced Dogtown hiker.

It's not like the old times, when the grazers kept it clipped; this was all low growth and boulders, and you got your bearings by climbing a rock and looking around. Today, few are the knolls that haven't gone to brush. Dogtown is a maze, fascinating but inscrutably challenging to the sense of direction.

Pack a picnic, a jacket in case of a shower or wind shift, strong walk- ing shoes, mosquito dope in summer, and something to pick blueber- ries into if they're ripe. Tell somebody your plans. Don't go alone. Wear bright clothing in the hunting season (between October and March). And bring a compass and the Dogtown Common Trail Map published by the Dogtown Advisory Committee.

About two hundred yards beyond the parking area, a left fork in the road at the nearly hidden Boulder 13 loops up through a pasture from which a path picks through the brush for fifty yards or so and wanders around three unmistakable boulders. One of these (map 5, 4) is part of a crumbled stone wall and has a natural toehold for a boost up that yields a rare Dogtown view of Squam River, West Parish, An- nisquam, the beaches, and the Bay.

Back on Dogtown Road, about across from Boulder 13 (map 5, 5), was the cellarless house of Esther Carter, a celebrated individualist dur- ing the decline of the village a hundred and seventy years ago. "Easter" was poor but proud, and scorned to live on berries as her neighbors did in the summer. "I eats no trash," she snorted; she cooked cab- bage dinners for the boys and girls from Riverdale and Squam who brought her food, and told their fortunes. Easter's was the only two- story home in Dogtown, and her second floor was occupied by "Old Ruth," thought to have been a freed slave. Old Ruth sometimes went

22. *Dogtown in the summer of 1922 provides a secluded picnic with a view. The writer's mother, second from right, is in an advanced primigravid state—with him.*

23. *Whale's Jaw, Dogtown, 1922. Dr. Joseph Garland, the writer's father-to-be, is on the jaw, his soon-to-be Aunt Betty on the snout.*

by the name of John Woodman and dressed in male clothing and performed manual labor, explaining merely that as a child she had to do both and got used to it.

Along this main street, once lined with humble houses and alive with humanity, the fugitive wind rustles the leaves of the oak and wild cherry. The gray rocks are all around, the stunted juniper, the spires of cedar, the bits of purple aster, the strange largesse of the blueberry bushes that spring from a ground as seemingly hard and dry as a neglected graveyard path, and the occasional bayberry shrub, so plentiful in the old times when this was all pasture that a contemporary newspaper account reported the rendering in the year 1858 alone of five hundred bushels of the tiny gray-green berries into a ton of candlewax.

In the pasture across the way from Boulder 18 was Molly Jacobs's place, marked by 19, but hard to find (map 5, 6), which Mann hints was of ill fame. Moll and her girl friends may have given their end of town a swinging reputation, but if they hastened its decline, they at least relieved the cheerlessness of it. After Molly's death, Cornelius Finson ("Black Neil," probably a freed slave) took over her cellar, convinced she had hidden treasure in it. They carried him down to the almshouse in the winter of 1830, starving and frostbitten, and he died a week later.

Dogtown is delusion.

A few paces along the path into Molly's pasture we can still make out the shallow carving on a rock to our left:

JAS. MERRY
DIED
SEPT. 18
1892

Fifteen paces farther in, barely legible on another:

FIRST
ATTACKED

The truth of what happened has been obscured by legend, but we do know James Merry's gored body was found near one of these rocks that Sunday morning, that the rocks were covered with blood, and that Patrick Nugent's bull, blood on one of his horns, was grazing nearby. Merry was sixty, a former fisherman, six feet three and in his prime one of the strongest men in Gloucester. His friends came up and carved these inscriptions.

Years later an account was published that Merry had been wrestling this bull since it was a calf the previous summer, staging bullfights for his friends, dressed in a makeshift matador's costume; that his adversary got too big for him; that they had to rescue Merry one day; and that after a drinking bout he came up here alone for a return match—and lost.

James Nugent, a son of the bull's owner, told the writer that one of the gang drinking down at Howard Blackburn's saloon the previous night challenged Merry, who had a reputation for his strength, that he couldn't top Johnny Carter's feat in tossing a calf by the tail over Squam bridge. Next morning Merry told his wife he was going berrying, but when he got to the pasture he left his boots and his bucket by the wall and tackled the bull, tried to throw it by the horns, and was gored straight through the heart.

Long afterwards—probably quite unaware of the bloody event— Roger Babson had his men carve on a nearby boulder:

NEVER TRY, NEVER WIN

Dogtown Square and Wharf Road

The air of obstinacy and delusion, of pathos and tragicomedy amidst grim subsistence that surrounded the decay of Dogtown seems to hang heaviest as we approach the crossroads of Dogtown Square, where pasture and stunted woods meet at Granny Day's Swamp (map 5, 7), a real slough of despond. One minute all is sun and breeze; the next, the feeling is of a stagnant bog, dank, dark, and dire.

At Dogtown Square the road splits before a phalanx of terminal moraine. Southeast, it splits again, one fork striking Eastern Avenue just over the Rockport line after three-quarters of a mile, the other (to the right and south) passing by Uncle Andrew's Rock (map 5, 8) in the pasture to wind on for some distance, in turn dividing east to the first mill site on Old Rockport Road and southwest to the Blackburn Industrial Park. This right-hand fork and its branches from Dogtown Square are not recommended to the casual hiker; the terrain is not remarkable, and the branches end remotely from the start.

The turn to take from here is left, due north through Granny Day's Swamp along a brush-threatened footpath called Wharf Road. Near Boulder 24, on the right, if we can locate it, stood a gambrel-roofed house, and in Historian John Babson's time, 1860, the cellar and foundations of the outbuildings were still there. Of it he wrote: "In 1814, this building was hardly habitable; and, in that year, its last tenant, Abraham Wharf, sought relief from poverty, and the accumulated sorrows of more than threescore and ten years, by putting an end to his existence, under a rock, where he had crawled for that purpose."

Granny Day made some claim to be a teacher. Her cellar is, or was years ago, submerged in a corner of her swamp where errant livestock, when this was common pasture, bogged down—occasionally, like the mastodons, for keeps.

Somewhere along Wharf Road, behind the brush to the eastward, is Boulder 25, marking the place of Peter Lurvey, the hero of Dogtown. On that August day of 1775, as Captain Lindsay attacked the harbor in the *Falcon*, Peter heard the alarm bell from the meetinghouse while huckleberrying with his wife on Pearce's Island. He kissed her, jumped in his dory, rowed across Squam River, raced up to his house here, grabbed his musket off the wall, and ran to the harbor to join the fray. With one other brave Gloucesterman, Peter Lurvey died by a British bullet.

Whale's Jaw

Wharf Road slithers between Dogtown Road, which brought us to the square, and the easterly end of the Commons Road, which was the extension of Gee Avenue before the Goose Cove Reservoir flooded the intervening low ground a few years ago. We head east on Commons Road, destination Whale's Jaw. After three hundred yards the trail swings north, by a boulder called Peter's Pulpit (map 5, 9) for no readily apparent reason, and descends into the ghoulish greenery of Brier Swamp. We have to keep an eye peeled for the left fork, which is identified by a metal culvert crossing the path forty feet in.

A short way on, back up into the pasture and the sunlight, there is—or for eons was, until recently—Whale's Jaw, a whale of a rock split agape ages ago by frost or lightning. In its prime, until someone built a campfire under the jaw in 1989, which broke it off, this most famous of Dogtown landmarks was a breeching Moby Dick about to clamp with an earthshaking snap on the leg of Captan Ahab.

If we're young and springy and well-sneakered, we scramble to the lip of the greater mandible, where a grand view should be the prize. The northeast path from Whale's Jaw comes out at the end of Squam Hill Road in Rockport, while the path northwest works around to Dennison Street and the north shore of Goose Cove.

Back in 1932 the Rockport police chief found himself in a bind over a pack of two hundred fifty wild pigs running loose on his end of Dogtown since several piggeries had been closed by the board of health some years earlier. A hiker complained that he'd been chased into a summer camp. Were they on private property and untouchable? The issue was resolved in the frying pan.

The Commons Road Walk

So much for the more common Dogtown hike. The alternate ramble of choice sets off from the Goose Cove Reservoir's Gee Avenue parking area. The reservoir is encircled by an excellent blacktop from which automobiles are excluded. We can walk in either direction and pick up on the opposite shore the old gravel Commons Road. It makes a pleasant and easy trip. We pass by sweet clumps of clethra on our way to Whale's Jaw, a jaunt of close to two miles, taking forty-five minutes if we spurn the beckoning high-bush blueberries.

Every Dogtown excursion has its twists. For example, we can enter by way of Dogtown and Wharf roads and return by Commons Road, thence clockwise around Goose Cove Reservoir to the path that proceeds south from the lower dam to Cherry Street, and south two hundred yards on Cherry to reenter the blacktop that returns us to the parking area.

Or we can press on from Whale's Jaw by the northwest path to Dennison Street, thence to Davis's millpond, and from here take the path that cuts back sharp left to the southeast through a brief brake of low brush to the reservoir's north dam, and back to either starting point.

Indeed, Dogtown offers you such a choice that with the Dogtown Common Trail Map in hand you may strike out across this mysterious heartland of Cape Ann and emerge almost wherever you choose— provided you know where you're going, and where you came from.

When Dogtown was closer to the deforested state in which the settlers left it, Thomas Wentworth Higginson described the scene in 1873 in *Oldport Days*:

I know of nothing like that gray waste of boulders; it is a natural Salisbury Plain, of which icebergs and ocean currents were the Druidic builders; in that multitude of couchant monsters there seems a sense of suspended life; you feel as if they must speak and answer to each other in the silent nights, but by day only the wandering sea-birds seek them, on their way across the Cape, and the sweet-bay and green fern imbed them in a softer and deeper setting as the years go by.

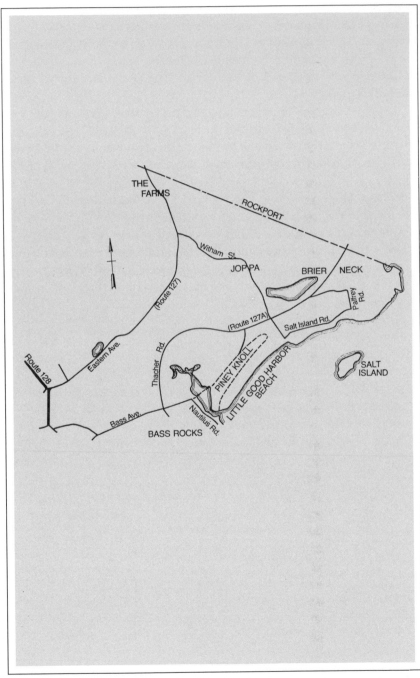

Map 6. The Farms to Little Good Harbor

CHAPTER 6

THE FARMS TO LITTLE GOOD HARBOR

Leave Main Street behind you and drive out Eastern Avenue from the Route 128 traffic lights, between the rows of well-kept Victorian houses. The small jewel of a pond on the left comes as a surprise on an August day when its pink water lilies are in bloom. The people out this way skate on it nights in the winter under lights. There was a larger pond directly across the road in former years, where the marsh is now, and Nat Webster filled an ice house from each.

From about here along to Rockport was, and still is to a few, "The Farms." Below the ridge that marks the edge of Dogtown and the highway, this was pretty good upland and pasture. On the sea side to the southeast was first-rate bottomland and salt hay marsh, in there back of Brier Neck and Little Good Harbor Beach.

There was good dirt here in The Farms after the plow broke the wildness of it, but it must have been the devil of a lonely place in those pioneer days before the timber was cut off. John Rowe hadn't been here five years when he was ready to unload the tract he'd bought in 1651, and he was the fourth owner since its granting in 1642. "If his wife were off his mind," he was quoted as raging, "he would set his house on fire and run away by ye light, and ye devil should take ye farm...he would live no longer among such a company of hellhounds"—for which outburst he was fined twenty shillings and directed to make public confession.

Joppa

Jeffrey Parsons fared better with his grant in 1685 of the lower land down toward Little Good Harbor Beach. Farmers, shore fishermen, and lobstermen the Parsonses were, and their tribe increased. Their land from Brier Neck to The Farms got to be known as Joppa, the road through it as Joppa Road. (Later the road's name was changed to

Witham Street, for Thomas Witham. He married a Babson girl at The Farms who brought him land for a dowry and gave him four daughters and seven sons for a bonus; six of their sons had sixty-four children between them.)

A Parsons who knew his Bible must have observed the striking similarity of Little Good Harbor to the ancient port of Joppa in Palestine (Jaffa today, now a southern section of Tel Aviv). Though open to the Mediterranean, the biblical port provided safe harbor for small boats behind the protection of an offshore reef of ledges. There is a plausible theory that in early colonial times our beach, equally open to the Atlantic, served a like purpose, and that behind it was a lagoon, a "little good harbor" for small boats—hence a "Joppa." The Newburyport Flats inside the mouth of the Merrimack River, incidentally, have been called Joppa too.

Most curiously, the Parsonses around here have been known colloquially for years as "Joppa Indians." Why Indians? But try this out: JOsePh PArsons.

Today there is no harbor here, good or little good. The beach suffices as one of the finest on the coast. Yet, but for man's ungovernable greed and obsession with tinkering with the landscape, "Joppy," as the natives call it, would even now be a busy little port on a very good little harbor indeed.

Little Good Harbor

The disappearance of Little Good Harbor parallels the fate that befell the Coffin farm when the trees were cut and the drifting dunes took over. How it happened here has been convincingly reconstructed by a former mayor, the late Dr. Elmer W. Babson.

When the Rowes and Parsonses penetrated the virgin land of The Farms and Joppa, there was no tidal creek at the Bass Rocks end of the beach as there is today. In its place, where the footbridge crosses, was an extension of the land over the site of Nautilus Road: a knoll about thirty feet high that narrowed markedly as it pushed on above the beach and terminated just short of Brier Neck. It was covered with trees, hence the Piney Knoll. Between the northeast end of it and Brier Neck coursed a substantial creek.

A large part of the present salt marsh, including the beach parking lot, was a lagoon that extended across Witham Street behind the Neck and embraced all that remains of it today, the freshwater pond. Small boats could pass from the open sea through the creek at Brier Neck (about where the public landing ramp is above the beach at the foot of Witham Street) and into the calm and protected waters of this shallow but undoubtedly good little harbor. Dr. Babson discovered this former topography on a 1781 British Admiralty chart. Brier Neck at an earlier stage in geological time must have been an island; the seas piled up sand all along the shore behind Long and Little Good Harbor beaches, making a barrier reef, which—in the case of Piney Knoll, anyway—was held in place by the roots of the trees. Niles Pond, farther down on Eastern Point, was probably created in like manner.

By 1750, as Babson reforged the chain of events, the settlers had cut down all those trees that anchored Piney Knoll. Reap the whirlwind. In 1757 came a three-day hurricane, talked of for a century. "The Great Storm" swept the top of Piney Knoll into the lagoon. Then, of course, wave and wind relentlessly eroded the knoll into the old harbor and slowly converted it to marsh. The creek at Bass Rocks didn't appear until about 1800. Some ten years later Dr. John Manning of Rockport purchased the entire original Rowe grant. Over a period of thirty years, looking to add to the salt marsh that was then the main source of cattle fodder, Dr. Manning filled in the Brier Neck creek and turned more than seven acres of Little Good Harbor into marsh. The thin trickle of the old creek was still there in 1830, but just barely.

How an ax can change destiny! Had they left the pines on Piney Knoll, Gloucester would have a nearly landlocked anchorage behind Little Good Harbor Beach and would have been spared the serious damage to the unprotected dunes wrought by the devastating winter storms of 1972 and 1978.

The Joppa Parsonses were pioneers at lobstering. They kept boats and pots at Salt Island, which you can cross to over the bar at low tide. No shortage then: in 1858 a cruising party off Cape Ann cut up lobster for flounder bait, and you could catch four hundred big ones a day from fifty pots. Twenty years later the Gloucester catch was 133,340 lobsters taken from 1,324 pots by fifty-three men in forty-eight dories. Back in 1818, one old timer reminisced, "a man could wade off at low water at Bass Rocks and catch any quantity of lobsters with a common gaff."

When the only way in was the long and dusty way by Eastern Avenue and Joppa Road, nothing disturbed that broad and bold Atlantic beach from Land's End in Rockport to Bass Rocks, broken only by Cape Hedge and Brier Neck, but the whoosh and slap of the surf, the mew of the gull, and the peep of the skittering sandpiper.

This splendid strand was boisterously breeched by the extension along Bass Avenue of the electric trolley branch to Long Beach, where in June 1895 the company proudly took the wraps off a pavilion, dance hall, restaurant, bowling alley, and vaudeville theater. Soon afterwards came the construction of Thacher Road over the old cart track above the shore. Thomas E. Babson described the joys of the Long Beach Branch: "The early type of open cars with single trucks were used on it. They had a habit of galloping like a horse. Guard bars were let down on both sides before crossing the trestle that carried the tracks over the sandy marsh behind Little Good Harbor Beach. Even so, a careless passenger was occasionally tossed off into the dunes."

Brier Neck and Salt Island

By 1905 Brier Neck was a squatters' paradise, festooned with the diminutive summer shacks of enthusiasts who staked their claims by right of first-come. Some time around 1909 Charles W. Luce, a smart Gloucester furniture dealer, succeeded in clearing the cloudy titles, bought up the property, and sold it off in lots restricted to the building of $2,000 cottages or better. The shacks were ordered off, and fine summer homes were put up with exciting views of Salt Island and the Atlantic, as we can see by proceeding left on Salt Island Road from the end of Witham Street, then left on Palfrey Road and left again back to Thacher Road, the shore route to Rockport.

Except for the possibility that there may have been an early salt works connected with it—perhaps an evaporating basin by the beach— Salt Island has never amounted to much save for decorating the view, which it has done very well. In the fall of 1919, though, it was the setting for a castle of wood and plaster created by Fox Films for some of the scenes of a fifteen-part thriller, *Bride 13*. The first castle was blown apart by an unscripted tornado and had to be rebuilt. Various attempts at rescuing a stunt man (disguised as the beleaguered heroine) from a lofty parapet with a hot air balloon went adrift, eventually landing all concerned in a brier patch on Brier Neck. The first try of the pirates to blow up the castle fizzled, but the second succeeded stupendously, and in an instant Salt Island was again just Salt Island.

24. *This Hollywood-style, fake-front castle on Salt Island was the scene of a chain reaction of mishaps that rivaled in excitement the script for the serial movie* Bride 13 *in 1919.*

The shining carriages of the nobby summer people whose "cottages" were strung out along the Back Shore clip-clopped regularly through The Farms after the Boston & Maine Railroad located a tiny depot for their convenience at Beaver Dam, a half a mile inside Rockport. After the Nugents bought farm land for their piggery, the straightaway was called the Nugent Stretch, and the short section of double track for the electric trolleys to pass each other coming and going was the Nugent Turnout.

The semiprofessional baseball games of the New England League at Webster's Field beside Cape Pond brought thousands of fans to the grandstand from as far as Boston. The Rockport White Sox were playing the Knights of King Arthur one day when the bleachers collapsed.

No one was seriously hurt, but one guy as he fell got hung up from an upright by his coat collar. Somebody shinnied up and cut him down with a pocket knife.

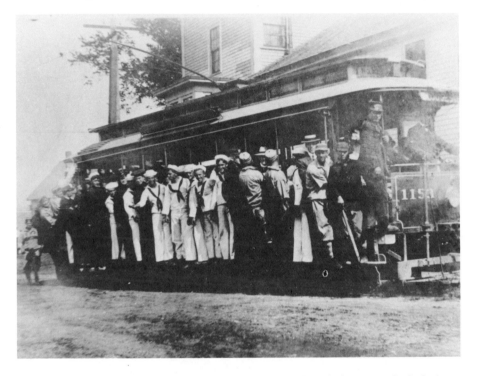

25. *The fleet's in Sandy Bay, it's April 16, 1906, and gobs and players jam the fresh-air trolley from Rockport's Dock Square for the semipro ballgame at Webster's Field.*

Ah, some of the greats played at Webster's—Ty Cobb and other occasional ringers from the majors, and a pair of Gloucester boys, John (Stuffy) McInnis from Warner Street, whose father was a teamster, and Cy Perkins from Centennial Avenue. Both went on to play for Connie Mack and the Philadelphia Athletics, among other teams, Stuffy as perhaps the greatest fielding first baseman of all time in spite of his five feet-eight, and Cy as a catcher.

Around 1909 or 1910 the state took over and widened Eastern Avenue. The job required broken rock for a base, and to get raw material for their portable crusher the workmen looked to the adjoining pastures. They would drill holes in the boulders, load and fuse them, and let young Dick Tarr, who lived there at The Farms, run out to hold up the trolley car if it came, while the boss dashed from rock to rock with his cigar. Once he touched off eighteen fuses that way before taking shelter.

So that was some excitement too, but mainly The Farms and Joppa have remained a quiet part of Gloucester where the natives have the long white beach to themselves in the long off-season and like it that way. As one old resident told the writer: "I don't know much about the other part of the earth." When asked what part she was referring to, she replied with a toss of her head: "Oh, over beyond Prospect Street, that way."

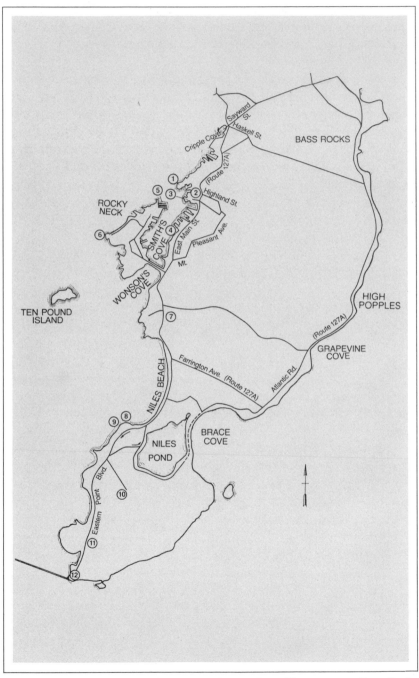

Map 7. East Gloucester to Bass Rocks

CHAPTER 7

EAST GLOUCESTER
to BASS ROCKS

Via Rocky Neck and Eastern Point

The sun rises and glows irresolutely through this East Gloucester thick o' fog. The glow breaks into patches of blue with the early morning warmth of spring, interspersed with fluffs by time for mug-up, and then the fog scales up, as they say. It lifts. Then, wherever this vast chunk of ledge hangs off Gloucester into the Atlantic Ocean, which is practically everywhere, the day sparkles.

Before the village here got so grand (after the railroad came from Salem in 1847) as to be called East Gloucester, the whole peninsula that makes the harbor was Eastern Point. It's a mile wide and two and a half long, as the herring gull flaps, from the head of Cripple Cove (a cripple is a swampy thicket) at the bottom of Point Hill, where East Main, Sayward, and Haskell streets collide, out to Dog Bar Breakwater. That's the length of Gloucester Harbor, in two parts. The Outer Harbor between the shores of Eastern Point and West Gloucester is a mile across and almost two long into Pavilion Beach. The Inner Harbor, "safe from all winds that blow," as an old almanac describes it, is a third of a mile across between waterfronts. That's a lot of harbor.

This whole peninsula is Cape Ann's cape, displaying the variety, the pockets of paradox, the successes and the failures of the greater Gloucester as on a stage. The important thing about it is the Atlantic Ocean. That's where it gets its fog, and its vitality.

East Main Street

Before the unlit monument that preceded the lighthouse at the end of Eastern Point was built in 1829, there was nowhere important for the road to go. This was all pasture, because the fishing industry didn't achieve greatness until the arrival of the railroad in 1847. Two years later Captain John Wonson's ferry connected East Gloucester and the main waterfront and took some of the business away from the land route, which wasn't dignified as East Main Street until the Great Fire of 1864 wiped out most of the downtown commercial district; at that point the old main stem was renamed from Front to Main Street.

Not much to look at today, but fifty years ago the waterfront from the Ben Smith Playground on Cripple Cove, where there is a high-tide public landing reached on foot, to the bend beyond Hammond Street was all Gorton-Pew Fisheries. In its glory as a salt-fish producer, Gorton's was a thumping, squeaking, grinding, steaming, chugging, sprawling combine of the Slade Gorton, John Pew, D. B. Smith, and Reed and Gamage companies that kept dozens of wharves and acres of flake yards busy with the unloading, filleting, salting, drying, boning, cutting, grinding, smoking, boxing, packaging, and canning of the millions upon millions of pounds of fish brought back from the North Atlantic banks by their fleets of handsome Gloucester schooners.

Along this part of East Main Street, Gorton's processed redfish during the boom that revived the lagging industry in World War II; it kept a smokehouse here, and a plant that turned out codfish cakes by the mile. Ah, that salt fish spread on the flakes, curing in the hot sun, gave off a pungency that in the recollection quickens the pulse and puts the veteran waterfront man in mind of schooners laying to the wharves, sails drying, and the thump-thump of handcarts over loose planks.

A few steps farther on, Norwood Court squeezes down to the water. When the codfish was king the neighbors referred to it as "Blubber Alley" in tolerant acknowledgment of the effusions from Joe Norwood's cod liver oil vats. Just beyond is the former Methodist Episcopal Church, described matter-of-factly in an 1896 guidebook as "within rifle shot" of the Baptist Chapel on Chapel Street.

Then we come to the massive cold storage and processing plants where millions of pounds of fish frozen into blocks, or "slabs," are landed by refrigerator freighters called "reefers" from Europe and as far off as Japan. Some of these imports are turned into frozen dinners on the spot; quantities are fanned out around the nation by an endless parade of refrigerator trailer trucks.

This once-famous wharf (map 7, 1) used to stockpile the fish preservative that served for three centuries before Clarence Birdseye perfected quick freezing here in Gloucester. Here was the warehouse of William

26. Due west from the summit of Hammond Street, Five Pound Island basks in the center of the Inner Harbor beyond the Slade Gorton wharves and flake yards for air-curing salt fish, 1912.

Parsons 2nd and Company, where towering salt barks and sometimes steamers from Sicily and Spain unloaded the stuff, over 32,000 tons of it in 1907, that made Gloucester the salt-fish capital of the world. These and the lumber carriers were among the last of the windships, a few square-riggers but mostly four- and five- and six-masted schooners; and their comings and goings, pulled and pushed by the churning, white-plumed harbor tugs, invested the port with an air of distant romance.

Two of these vessels, the full-rigged ship *John Bunyan* and the bark *Sandy Hook*, were unloading on December 10, 1872, as a terrific gale pounded the coast and whacked and banged their heavy hulls against the Parsons wharf. Suddenly the entire wharf and warehouse collapsed with a thunderous crash, and 10,000 hogsheads of Cadiz salt plummeted into the harbor, taking with them forty tons of fish.

The west jetty of this wharf during Prohibition in the 1920s was a Coast Guard base from which many a rumrunner was brought to heel—and to which many a patrol boat returned emptyhanded.

Down behind the small business block, now a parking lot, was the wharf from which the late Captain Albert Arnold and his sons pursued the gillnet fishing that he introduced here in 1910. That was a comeuppance for Gloucester. Captain Arnold and other Great Lakes fishermen from Charlevoix, Michigan, brought their boats and gear

for a try at the sea. Ocean gillnetting had been attempted years before, not successfully. The Michigan fleet increased to nearly forty-five
vessels, however, and entire wharves were given over to the picturesque reels still used today for drying, cleaning, and repairing the
long nets. But there are fewer fish out there, and the work is hard;
now only a handful of gillnetters are left, among them the same *Phyllis
A* built by Captain Arnold in 1925. She is still in his family, one of the
oldest active fishing vessels in America.

27. *Horse-drawn omnibus
and driver, petticoated
ladies, town pump, and
flagpole with nautical
topmast and crosstrees
say it's East Gloucester
Square in the 1870s.*

Before the Square (map 7, 2) had a town pump in it and a horse-
drawn omnibus that vibrated folks back and forth to town, the main
road dusted its way up Highland Street, then along the heights as Mt.
Pleasant Avenue, descending back to the harbor below Isaac Patch's
ice pond and above the causeway to Rocky Neck. There wasn't solid
land enough to put a road along the bypassed section between the
ledges and Smith's Cove (named for John Smith, who owned land
around here in the seventeenth century) until fill was dumped, and
perhaps some ledge removed as well, probably around the 1840s.
    Down Pirate's Lane is a spacious filled-in wharf (map 7, 3). From
the public landing in the small cove by the street Captain Wonson first
rowed his passengers across to Duncan's Point in 1849. Then there
were various small steam ferries and the Douglasses' sailboat when

28. *The steam ferry* Little Giant *puffs from ''over town'' into the East Gloucester landing past Gorton-Pew's Reed and Gamage wharf (Beacon Marine Basin today). Eben Parsons snapped his shutter at exactly 5:10 p.m., March 4, 1911, according to his careful record.*

the weather favored. Finally a narrow trestle walk was built three hundred and seventy-five feet between the wharves for access to the tiny steamer *Little Giant,* of which there is a model in the Cape Ann Historical Museum. On demand the ferry touched at Tarr's Wharf off the end of Rocky Neck. The fare remained four cents for years.

The summer gallery of the North Shore Arts Association occupies the cavernous warehouse on this wharf. The association acquired the building in 1922 from Thomas E. Reed, who had a stevedoring firm and kept the steam lighters *Abbott Coffin* and *Phillip.* Salvatore Santapaola had charge of *Phillip* when it later served as the city's fireboat. Salvy always kept steam up but wasn't on hand the day some young fellows towed a burning launch alongside, jumped aboard, aimed the hose, and twirled away at the valve—but got no water.

Hearing the commotion, Salvy came running, ducked below, and spun a second valve on the steam engine. A jet shot from the nozzle, kicked the boys pants over teakettle, and struck the flaming boat with such impact that it capsized and sank on the spot, just as Salvy was poking his head up to give instructions.

Tradition marks the Arts Association wharf as the one from which Captain Andrew Robinson in 1713 launched a two-masted vessel, perhaps a modification of the traditional design hereabouts, that supposedly slid so slickly into the water as to inspire an onlooker to exclaim, ''See how she scoons!''—upon which the builder declared, ''A scooner let her be!'' Schooners they have been ever since, although the actual genesis of the winged craft that brought fish and fame to Gloucester is enmeshed in the folklore of boat design. Appropriately, the site is a high-tide public landing.

29. *No space is wasted curing salt fish on the wooden flakes at Reed and Gamage on East Main Street, now Beacon Marine Basin. The year is 1912. The steam ferry slip is behind the flakes on the roof at right. In the ''Deep Hole'' anchorage, a salt bark, probably from Sicily, dries sails.*

Next along is the Beacon Marine Basin, a picturesque mix of wharves for commercial and pleasure craft, a do-it-yourself boatyard, a machine shop, and apartments. Reed and Gamage and Amos Story and, later, Booth Fisheries landed vessels here. Booth had flake yards up to the sidewalk when John Alexander, a cabin boy of sixteen from the Azores, stepped off a whaling ship at New Bedford in 1908. He came to Gloucester's Portuguese colony, worked as a gardener, became a fish peddler, saved his money, leased the southwest corner of the Booth wharf, built a small fish store and smokehouse, and with the help of the local girl he married built up a business that enabled him to buy the entire Beacon Marine property.

An attraction in the Beacon dock for years has been the white a hundred and thirty-three foot *Coronet*, a schooner yacht built in 1885. Winner of a race to Ireland two years later, veteran of at least three voyages around the world and five around Cape Horn, she was magnificent under full sail in her time. In 1905 she was acquired by a religious group that took her on several missionary voyages, the last of which was shrouded in tragic mystery; the church still owns and maintains her.

From bluff Banner Hill overlooking Beacon Marine Basin (so named after the Wonson brothers raised a flag there at the outbreak of the Civil War), it was a Gloucester tradition every old-time Christmas Eve to torch off a tar barrel on Bonfire Rock "to drive Santa Claus from hiding."

30. *The "electric" dashes along East Main Street toward Rocky Neck on a sunny June 4, 1911. A derelict schooner dies in the dock. A seine boat lies on the John F. Wonson wharf. Across Smith Cove is the Rocky Neck Marine Railway.*

Beyond Beacon Marine, the Morse and A&M wharves (map 7, 4) are a living museum of the old-time Gloucester fisheries. Down here a few tenacious individualists hang on to dragging, gillnetting, line trawling, tuna fishing, and lobstering in the tradition of the John F. Wonson Company, which for fifty years sent a fleet of twenty schooners from these wharves to follow the fish from the Delaware Capes to Greenland. The long frame building on the street, hiked up partly on piles, was the carpentry and boat shop. Up on the outside east wall was nailed a stuffed sea serpent, with a sign informing the credulous tourist where and how it was caught; unique features of the species were its wooden head and cork body covered with canvas.

31. *When George Marble Wonson built his barn up Marble Street in East Gloucester in 1883, he meant BARN. His carts hauled stone ballast from the Back Shore for the fishing schooners at the East Gloucester wharves. The barn burned in 1977.*

Before the house at 265 East Main Street was built, the lot was owned by Herbert and John Wennerberg, who supplied the fishing fleet with fresh water. From their stone reservoir in the south corner of the front yard a gravity pipe slanted out over Smith Cove on a trestle. When a schooner wanted water, the cook would run up a bucket in the rigging, the summons to the Wennerbergs to come alongside in their cat-rigged waterboat *Wanderer* and fill 'er up.

Next beyond, the cavernous brick Twin Light Garage, dating back almost to the invention of the automobile, has traded repairs for repertoires and is home to the Gloucester Stage Company, which provides year-round theater and an acting school for the North Shore.

Rocky Neck

No one knows when the causeway to Rocky Neck was raised above the tide, but it must have been at least a hundred and fifty-five years ago. When it was Peter Mud's Neck in the 1600s, you had to get there "across the bar" at low water. Today there's a public park on the Outer Harbor side of the bar and a parking lot above Smith Cove; in the busy season it's a good idea to park there and cross on foot as Mr. Mud did. This isolated sheep pasture of yore is now jammed with homes, narrow and winding streets, art studios and galleries, gift shops, marinas and restaurants, and precious little street room. Dredging of the Smith Cove flats, public docks, and a ramp with access from the parking lot are planned.

Yet this quasi-island retains its oldest industry, the colorful and roughhewn marine railways at the end of Rocky Neck Avenue (map 7, 5), which from 1859 until about 1970 employed a steam engine to haul up the fishing vessels for painting and repairs. The landmark marine antifouling copper paint manufactory of Tarr and Wonson, built at the Neck's western tip in 1863 (map 7, 6), ceased operations in the early 1980s. It has a fine harbor view, but the access road is narrow and the parking restricted, so leave your car behind. For years the 1851 bell from the former Point Grammar School on Plum Street struck the hour from "the copper paint" until it was moved again to the roof of the Gloucester Bank and Trust Company across the water on Rogers Street.

In 1859 the Neck had a population of a hundred and forty-three and was mainly sheep pasture. But in the years after the Civil War its Smith Cove shore came to rival the East Gloucester side as every running foot of protected deep-water wharfage was pressed into the service of the expanding fleet. The relics of that era, thick with the smell of fish and salt, were long since converted to the uses of the artist, the summer boarder, and the tourist, a trend that began with the discovery of the Neck's quaint beauty by such painters as Walter L. Dean, A. W. Buhler, Victor Valenkamph, Frank Duveneck, Childe Hassam, John Sloan, John Henry Twachtman, Charles Gruppe, Frederic Mulhaupt, and their friends and followers.

Rocky Neck semiofficially acknowledged the irreversibility of change with Captain Frank Foster's conversion of the homestead of his in-laws, the Rackliffes, into the Rockaway House in 1896. The East Gloucester Yacht Club was organized the same year at the Head of the Harbor, and the gala opening of its new clubhouse on Wiley Street in 1901 (still there, privately owned) helped lay to rest the good old days when the

Neckers had it all to themselves. The final shattering of the insular peace came in the 1890s with the clattering electric trolleys that disgorged the outside world at the junction of Rocky Neck Avenue and Wonson Street.

Bluff and on the edge of the channel, the northwest shore of the Neck was ill adapted to the berthing of vessels except at Colonel Charley Fred Wonson's Gloucester Salt Fish Company, topped eighty years ago by a windmill that probably kept a water tank filled; the structure is now the apartment complex of West Wharf.

Next to the marine railways was Rocky Neck's third landmark, the Gloucester School for the Theater. From 1919 to 1950 the beloved "Little Theater" (made over from Tarr's paint shop) was New England's premier summer drama shrine under the inspired direction of Florence Cunningham, a Gloucester girl who was later a sought-after speech coach in Hollywood.

The trolleys and the Little Theater have come and gone. Back in 1911 the sympathetic correspondent for the *North Shore Breeze* was lamenting that the strangers and their bungalows were elbowing out the homes of the natives "with their heaped-up yards in which repose old dories, lobster pots, fishing gear and such equipment of the shore fisherman. The stranger likes this picturesqueness, but not so the old fisherman. He clings to the olden days. These radical changes almost make him weep. He is oftentimes seen lost in contemplation of the 'curse' that has overtaken Rocky Neck."

One man's curse, of course, may be another's blessing, and all the world is invited early every July to the annual jubilee of the art colony culminating in its sometimes raucous Beaux Arts Ball.

The Road to Eastern Point

From Rocky Neck, East Main Street transforms itself into Eastern Point Road, curving by Wonson's Cove, almost as cozy as ever, where Samuel de Champlain and his men landed (and a public landing it has remained ever since) for a drink from possibly the very stream that flows now under the road. In the winter of 1989 some twenty or more mute swans graced the cove's shore with their stately presence.

Past the sites of impressionist John Henry Twachtman's studio and the summer Harbor View Hotel, where Princeton President Woodrow

Wilson and Mrs. Wilson stayed and enjoyed the view, we climb Patch's Hill. Old Isaac Patch, whose farm and pasture spanned Eastern Point from sea to harbor, and his neighbors, old George Marble Wonson, hauled ballast stone for the vessels to the wharves by oxcart from Grapevine Cove and High Popples Beach.

From the heights up here Ten Pound Island comes in and out of view. No wonder the French discoverer exclaimed "Beauport!" that September day of 1606 before sailing away to avoid any unpleasantness with the local redskinned landowners. The ship *Talbot*, bound from England for Salem with settlers, anchored in our harbor on June 27, 1629, and sent four men to this tiny island in a boat; they "brought back again ripe strawberries and gooseberries and sweet single roses." Fifteen years later the new town voted that this island "shall be reserved for Rams onlie; and whoever shall put on anie but great Rams shall forfelt 2s. 6d. per head." Those ten pounds, then, were probably sheep pounds, or pens, not sterling paid to the Indians, as tradition has it.

The lighthouse on Ten Pound Island was lit in 1821. In the summer of 1880 Winslow Homer boarded with the keeper and painted fifty entrancing watercolors of the encircling harbor. The United States Fish Hatchery started hatching fish and lobster here in 1889 and was joined in 1925 for ten years by the pioneer operational Coast Guard air station in the country, hatching plans to catch the rumrunners. Base 7 grew from a small scout plane, an Army canvas hangar, and two men to two amphibians, a scout, a hangar blasted out of the ledge, and seventeen men under the founder of the service, Lieutenant Commander Carl C. von Paulsen.

In 1956 the last keeper left, and the light was replaced by an adjacent automatic signal. The next year Washington gave the island back to Gloucester. In 1989 lighthouse preservationists restored the familiar flashing red to the 1881 brick tower, marking the two hundredth anniversary of the Coast Guard. You're free to go there for a picnic if you can get there.

Beyond the crest of Patch's Hill, at the south corner of Grapevine Road, is the summer cottage and studio of Childe Hassam with its graceful roof. Farther along on the right, condominiums occupy the site of the multicottaged and enormously popular Hawthorne Inn. "White-capped nurses or nattily attired bicyclists are enjoying the beauty and restfulness of this shady, vernal road,'' wrote one Gay Nineties habitue, which was just the atmosphere genial George Stacy took pains to create in his joyous sprawl of a dozen buildings and more, with casino, vaudeville, dancing, games, boating, and concerts by German contraltos on tour. The inn was the vortex of the East Gloucester colony. ''Matches are not made in heaven, my dear,'' aspiring mothers-in-law clucked knowingly at their daughters, ''but at the Hawthorne Inn.''

32. A. S. Parker sails his Swampscott dory past the Hawthorne Inn, July 8, 1911. Eben Parsons caught it from another boat.

Among all the summer boardinghouses and hotels, there is satisfaction for sentimentalists in the survival of the first, the old, brown Fairview Inn, set back from Eastern Point Road on the left (map 7, 7). The Fairview was opened by Mrs. Mary Wonson in 1842 and in its time was host to Louisa May Alcott, to artists Stephen and Maxfield Parrish, and in 1894 and 1895 to Rudyard Kipling and his family while the Bard of Empire soaked up Gloucester lore for his great sea novel *Captains Courageous.*

Eastern Point

The Gate Lodge of friendly but firm design erected at the bend by the syndicate that in 1887 bought the Niles Farm marks the beginning of

33. From 1904 until it burned in 1908, George Stacy's Colonial Arms dominated Eastern Point and the Outer Harbor. In the trees at left is the Niles farmhouse.

34. Edwardian summer elegance and ease at its most elevated. The porte cochere of the Colonial Arms.

this private domain, initially of summer estates. Niles Beach is open to the public, however, and sweeps along invitingly ahead.

On summer weekends and holidays the Association of Eastern Point Residents stations a constable at the stone pillars half along Niles Beach to monitor the traffic over Eastern Point Boulevard. Eastern Point roadways give access to the Breakwater and the Audubon Society sanctuary to the capacity of the parking space below the lighthouse. The roads are open to visitors by bicycle or on foot.

The estate behind the masonry wall on the curve at the far end of Niles Beach is on the site of the Eastern Point farmhouse that burned to the ground in 1909. The first to till this land was Samuel Stevens, two hundred and seventy years ago; the last was Thomas Niles, the writer's great-great-grandfather, who bought his four hundred acres in 1844 for $12 an acre. Fifteen years after his death Farmer Niles's numerous heirs sold his dream of "gentlemen's seaside estates" for $250 an acre to a syndicate that built the first eleven summer cottages in 1889. Today's acre has increased a thousand fold in price and more.

In 1908, on New Year's Night, a spectacular fire destroyed George Stacy's most romantic creation. He had sunk $230,000 into his colossal Colonial Arms (map 7, 8) only four years earlier. Three hundred rooms embraced the shore with five-story arms from the fulcrum of a portico four stories high, in the bosom of which nestled a porte-cochere of elegance. For all of three hundred feet this magnificent summer hotel swept around the ledge now occupied by the second and third cottages of stone beyond the beach. The Colonial Arms provided Stacy with four solidly booked seasons, and Eastern Pointers with something to talk about, before it all went up in smoke and flames people claimed they could read their newspapers by on Pavilion Beach, a mile and a half across the harbor.

Beauport

Behind the next stone wall is a monument to a different kind of ego. Beauport is the magical architectural collage that the interior decorator and pioneer in fashionable Americana, Henry Davis Sleeper, put together over a period of years, beginning with the starkly simple insides of the early eighteenth-century Cogswell House he transplanted from Essex in 1907 (map 7, 9). Once started, Sleeper's obsession grew on him until he ran out of land. By then he was the curator of a personal museum of forty rooms, each a moody tour de force of his own manipulation of period, dimension, object, color, and the shimmering reflections from the harbor below his scores of windows. After his death in 1934, Sleeper's Beauport was purchased by Mrs. Helena Woolworth McCann, daughter of the retail magnate; and on hers it was presented by her children to the Society for the Preservation of New England Antiquities. Beauport is open to the public Monday through Friday, 10:00 to 4:00, May 15 to October 15, and on weekends in addition from September 15 to October 15.

Tree-shaded Fort Hill Avenue, true to its promise, comes out on a brush-grown old fort (map 7, 10). In 1863 the government built this earthworks on Farmer Niles's best field and armed and manned it with seven thirty-two-pounders and an artillery company in rather an over-reaction to the burning of six Gloucester schooners on Georges Bank by a Confederate raider that June. The fort, which remained unnamed because the politicians couldn't agree whom to name it for, was a camp ground for a few weeks during the Spanish War, when the state militia were dispatched to protect Gloucester from the Spanish Navy in the summer of 1898. That winter the height of Eastern Point it crowned was bought by Cleveland railroad tycoon Henry C. Rouse, who erected within the old earthworks The Ramparts, a hospitable Tudor fortress that reigned over the Point until 1950, when all but the stone towers was razed by the owners.

The private pier at the end of Wharf, or Raymond's, Beach was built about 1836 for loading granite from a quarry in back on schooners for Boston to build, for instance, the foundation of its Customs House in 1847. Fifty yards beyond here on the left, a path ducks into the twenty-six acres of the Eastern Point Wildlife Sanctuary (map 7, 11), given to the Massachusetts Audubon Society in 1961 by the late brothers S. Edward and Jonathan S. Raymond, heirs to The Ramparts property. An enchanting, tiger-colored flurry of far-fluttering monarch butterflies and a great variety of birds pause at this wild refuge of land in the Atlantic on their annual migrations.

Lighthouse, Breakwater, and Mother Ann

In colonial days a sentinel grove of oaks marked the end of Eastern Point for mariners. This succumbed to time and tempest, and in 1829 the federal government bought an acre and built a stone day beacon, to which a whale oil lamp and a cottage for Keeper Samuel Wonson were added two years later. The lighthouse was built anew on its old foundation in 1848; it was rebuilt in 1890 as it is today, fifty-seven feet above sea level, visible on a clear night thirteen miles (map 7, 12). The revolving lantern and fog bell were first operated by hand-wound clockworks. These gave way to electric motors. A bell was added to the wooden light structure on the far end of Dog Bar Breakwater. Then a radio beacon by the lighthouse. The bells were replaced by electronic horns whose bleats combine in a doleful chorus with the sighs of Mother Ann's Cow, the whistling buoy to the southward. In 1985 everything was automated, and the lighthouse cottage, after a hundred and fifty-four years of occupation by a succession of faithful keepers, was converted to quarters for personnel from the Coast Guard station up in the harbor.

The Breakwater, long agitated for, was built 2,250 feet over Dog Bar by the Army Engineers as Congress doled out the funds between 1894 and 1905. Before the granite foundation broke high water, nearly forty

35. A gothic wood engraving of 1875 catches the Eastern Point Light's stark sentinel quality as no photograph could.

confused sailing vessels came to grief on it, some forever. Open from sunup to sundown in calm weather, it's an exciting walk out into the middle of the harbor and a favorite spot for fishing for flounder, mackerel, and pollock. When the swells are breaking over it thirty or forty feet high in the fury of an easterly gale, and the whistler shrieks its distress, it hardly needs mentioning that Dog Bar Breakwater is closed to the public.

Around on the back side of the lighthouse ledge reclines Mother Ann, buxom but Puritan in profile, a stone visage familiar to Gloucester people on land and sea. She may be viewed (with due regard for the owners) from the end of the private driveway past the stone wall fronting Mother Ann's Cottage.

Niles Pond and Brace Cove

Returning, we follow Lake Avenue counterclockwise around Niles Pond, a placid, inland kind of pond we might expect to find in Goshen or North Bellingham, with its water lilies and dragonflies and banks of laurel; its loosestrife, goldenrod, and tansy; its swans, waterfowl, and lurking snappers; and its flying iceboats and hockey pucks of January. But when we come out on the narrowest of causeways, what do we discover to our amazement and delight but the Atlantic Ocean, twenty feet away! The contrast couldn't be more striking: a bucolic "great pond" on one side, the sea crashing—or whispering, according to its mood—into the perfect ellipse of Brace Cove on the other, guarded by the giant hulk of Brace Rock, the subject to which Fitz Hugh Lane returned again and again in his later years.

From our vantage it dawns on us that we're standing on a barrier reef, that the pond was not too long ago a lagoon inevitably sealed off by the rising mound of sand and gradually freshened by springs and rainfall.

There is no counting Brace Cove's toll. Strange to say, most of the ill-starred craft it has claimed steered a course in here, guided by the cries of lookouts who believed, as they peered across the flatness of the cove and the pond beyond on a dark night or foggy day, before trees and houses had sprouted on the western side of the pond, that they were farther on, safely rounding the end of Eastern Point. Thus the northeast headland of Brace Cove (brace: an inlet) was cursed in the days of sail as the "False Point." And thus with good reason did the Massachusetts Humane Society maintain a barn-red surfboathouse on Brace's north shore and a volunteer crew of local mariners at the ready with stout boat, long oars, strong backs, and breeches buoy.

Leaving this fragile membrane, we can go left on Bemo Avenue and come out on the harbor, or keep around Brace Beach to the False Point and the start of Atlantic Road, a shore drive of nearly two miles that for the pure and elemental feel of the ocean it gives cannot be rivaled anywhere short of the Maine coast.

The Back Shore

The whole of what the settlers called Eastern Point appears to have been a forest when they found it. After it was cut over, most of the Point from Brace Cove to Bass Rocks, the Back Shore, went to common pasture and seems never again to have reverted to timber. Many of these "cow rights" north of Thomas Niles's Eastern Point farm were bought up by his neighbor Isaac Patch, with whom Niles spent years successfully fighting Ike's alleged trespasses on his beach after sea moss for fertilizer. The Patches didn't sell off to the Fassetts and the Looses for their summer mansions near Grapevine Cove until around eighty years ago. Before that the Back Shore was all wild and moorish and useless except for fowling, berrying, fishing for striped bass, taking stones for ballast, and watching the seas, and now and then a vessel, crash on the rocks.

It's a mighty, smashing, lashing coast here in a storm. The gale-driven swells heave in to breach the shoals in cauldrons of mad white water before dashing on the rocks in a continuous roar, heavy with menace, that raises goose pimples for miles downwind. Beyond Grape-vine Cove a half a mile is High Popples, a sloping-off of abraded stones, round and smooth, mistakenly supposed by some to be "popples." But no, a popple is literally a heaving of water over stones, and that is what the surf does here, heaving on the surge, and on the under-tow raking and rattling and poppling the rounded rocks.

36. *After the death in 1870 of George Rogers, porches were added to his house, and as the Bass Rocks Inn it presided for a while over the summer colony Gloucester's Great Mover founded on the Back Shore.*

Bass Rocks

As Ike Patch was making hay in the Great Pasture, so was George H. Rogers, that interesting and imaginative Gloucester merchant of the Surinam trade who commenced in 1845 a systematic harvest of cow rights in the Harbor and Sayward pastures behind and south of the small headland above Little Good Harbor Beach known as Bass Rocks. Rogers sank a fortune in his land, laboring to bring it under cultivation, laying out his own summer estate, scratching out roads, building cottages—and moving them. He was one of those compulsive Gloucester building movers. He acquired the Methodist Church on Prospect Street that was being replaced—the one they called "The Old Sloop"—and brought it up here, whole or in parts, for his barn. About 1850 he bought a handsome brick bowfront residence at the corner of Washington and Summer streets in Boston (where Filene's is today), said to have been designed by the noted Boston architect Charles Bul-

37. Porches open to the gale-driven spray, Judge Sherman's chained-down cottage presided with stubborn grace over Good Harbor Beach and a less-fortunate work of man. A hundred years later it's still there, though enclosed.

finch, rolled the house onto a barge, sailed it to Gloucester, and rolled it ashore at Cripple Cove. Apparently Rogers hoped to move this gem to Bass Rocks, but the story has it that the Haskell Street hill was just too steep, and he left his Boston brick at the bottom of the slope on East Main Street, where today it adds grace to the corner.

In the end, his reach exceeded his grasp, and George Rogers died broke in 1870. His Bass Rocks dream passed into the hands of Henry Souther of Boston. Lots were sold, a golf course was carved out, and hotels were built—those breezy arks of a more carefree day. To one of Souther's associates, Judge Edgar J. Sherman of Lawrence, fell perhaps the choicest lot. Sherman quite literally bolted his aerie to the peak of Bass Rock itself, where it still commands the Back Shore of Gloucester, cupola and all, just as it did the day John Webber paid a visit in 1885:

The scene from the spacious veranda of this dwelling is a grand one— to the left is noticed the long white sandy strip of Little Good Harbor Beach; on our right the noble old ocean stretches out in its grandeur to the sky; Salt Island and Thacher's lie directly in front of us, the two tall lighthouses on the latter rising like grim sentinels above the vasty deep; while 70 odd feet beneath us the "sad sea waves" dash with terrific force against the huge jagged rocks, sending a thick blanket of snow-white foam afar over the restless surface of the little cove.

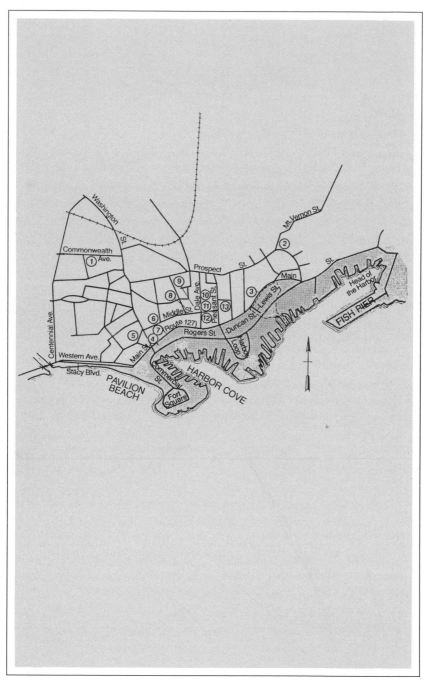

Map 8. Downtown

CHAPTER 8

DOWNTOWN

There's a gale upon the waters and there's foam upon the sea,
And looking out the window is a dark-eyed girl for me,
And driving her for Gloucester, maybe we don't know
What the little ones are thinking when the mother looks out so.
— "The Seiners," James B. Connolly

If the blood of Gloucester is the sea and its soul the waterfront, then its heart is downtown, where a person could live near enough to catch sight from an upstairs window of a vessel rounding Eastern Point, with someone on board whose impending arrival made the pulse beat faster.

Downtown has always been on the sea but never quite of it. It is the expansion of the original Harbor Village back of the wharves to the high ground between Governor's Hill on the west and Portuguese, or Portagee, Hill on the east—give or take a little to avoid an argument.

The oldest and most architecturally distinctive part of downtown, give or take a little, was approved by the city and state as an historic district in 1977, thereby holding the integrity of the exterior appearance of all structures to strict standards.

Governor's Hill

This height was more obviously commanding before homes were built upon it, and its dominance merited for it the honor of being named after the highest office in the colony some time during the early days of settlement. It's at the top of Commonwealth Avenue, appropriately, and we get up here from either Centennial Avenue or Washington Street (map 8, 1).

The summit is shared by a city park of sorts, merely an old pasture, and by the enviably situated home whose widow's walk during World War II enclosed an air raid lookout. The views of city, harbor, sea, and bay are glorious.

Small wonder that on April 16, 1776, the newly self-liberated Massachusetts General Court ordered beacons placed here and at Marblehead, Boston, and Blue Hill in Milton, to be lit in all haste upon the first sight of a British gunboat off the coast. For years after, Governor's Hill was known also as Beacon Pole Hill, and the rusted bits of iron fittings in drillholes in the ledge perhaps stayed the lofty beacon against the buffets of the gale.

Three parallel and backward-sweeping roads sufficed the Harbor Village then. With their accustomed directness the settlers called them Front (now Main) Street, Middle Street (originally Cornhill), and Back Street, later divided into High and Prospect streets. Back of Back Street was the harbor swamp, which they didn't get around to reclaiming until they needed the land much later.

Prospect Street

Descending Governor's Hill to Washington Street, we direct our steps east on Prospect Street and find little of an antique nature left on it today. The windmill erected in the year 1732 on the block between School and Church streets is long gone. For another hundred years this prominence was Windmill Hill, but the good work for which the vanes whirled is forgotten. The ground was occupied from 1864 to 1947 by the Collins School.

Beyond Maplewood Avenue is the seat of Gloucester's first Roman Catholic parish, St. Ann's. The rectory is about where the colonial Garrison House was. This is the scene of the tale of Peg Wesson. The Gloucester militia who were about to depart for the siege of Louisburg in Nova Scotia in 1745 are said to have been quartered here and to have teased Peg because some of the neighbors said she was a witch. She threatened to put the hex on them.

A few weeks later at Louisburg a crow appeared in their camp, an ill omen, obviously Peg in disguise. Since nothing less than silver could fell a witch, one sharpshooter loaded his musket with a sleeve button and brought the bird to earth. Back home after the campaign, the soldiers learned that Peg Wesson had fallen at that very moment with a broken leg, and when she was examined, out popped a silver sleeve button.

Some of the first Irish in Gloucester after the Famine lived in this section, among them John and Catherine Brennan in the old Garrison House, he fishing and working the gravel pit in back, herself teaching the ABCs in her cellar room to the neighborhood kids, including future mayor Sylvy Whalen and Jack Flaherty, one of the two Gloucestermen ever on the Superior Court.

It was in the home of John Dooly at the top of Reynard Street, edge of Dogtown, that the first mass in Gloucester was celebrated, New Year's Day, 1849. The Irish and the Portuguese made do until 1871, when they got their first settled pastor, Father Luigi Acquarone. His tireless successor, Father J. J. Healy, was the priest who put the parish on its feet and raised the money to build St. Ann's Church, which took ten years from cornerstone to consecration in 1886.

Franklin Square boxes the southwest corner of Prospect and Pleasant streets but was India Square a hundred and seventy-five years ago, named for the business engaged in by John Somes and Elias Davis, who had homes here and were leading spirits in the India Company. They sent the *Winthrop and Mary*, a remarkably small vessel of a hundred and five tons, on two voyages to Calcutta; she was never heard from after clearing Sumatra, homeward bound from her third, in 1800.

Mt. Vernon Street curves up Portuguese Hill, the highest on the east side of town, long the precinct of the brave and hardy fishermen who from 1845 on rejuvenated Gloucester with the salty blood of the Azores. The houses up here are trim and close together, bright in the sunlight, most of them with a vista of the shining harbor far below that must have reminded the first-generation occupants of the slopes of home. It is these houses that captivated and were immortally captured by the artist Edward Hopper. Beyond and up Perkins Street, the aspect shifts to Little Good Harbor Beach, the sea beyond, and beyond that, dreams of Fayal and Flores and Santa Maria.

The Azoreans and later the continental Portuguese shared the forecastle with Gloucester's other deep-water fishermen. That day is largely past, and their descendants are more given now to shore pursuits, though a few moved out and keep the tradition alive on the West Coast.

The Portuguese community organized a parish of its own in 1890 under The Reverend Francis U. De Bem and built its first church two years
later. That building was destroyed by fire in 1914 and replaced in 1915
with the arresting, sandy stucco of the Church of Our Lady of Good
Voyage (map 8, 2), designed after the church on the Azorean island
of San Miguel. The striking ten-foot statue of Our Lady between the
towers, cradling a Gloucester schooner, is a reproduction of the original commissioned by A. Piatt Andrew and given in 1915 to the new
church for which he led the fundraising effort; found to be decayed
beyond repair in 1984, the upper part of the old statue was placed in
the Cape Ann Historical Museum. The first modern carillon in America
was installed in the towers in 1922.

How evocative of Gloucester is the interior, of the grandeur and
cruelty of the sea, and of the Old World faith of the builders of this
inspiring shrine of the fishermen, built with the coin of the deep! Mysterious and moving—the blue of the sky and the blue of the sea in the
Sanctuary, the ship models aloft by the Stations of the Cross, more
eloquent in their way than any prayer.

One of those men of faith was Captain Joseph P. (Smoky Joe)
Mesquita. In 1902 he introduced from the old country the Festival of
the Crowning, making good on his vow when he and his crew were
rescued in a seeming miracle from the foggy waters of Georges Bank
after their schooner *Mary Mesquita* was sent to the bottom by the
Cunarder *Saxonia*. That old and most colorful ceremony of thankful-
ness culminates on Pentecost Sunday in spring with a parade from
Our Lady to the home of the man chosen by lot to be crowned "Im-
perator" from among the members of the Portuguese-American D.E.S.
Club across Prospect Street. The initials stand for *Divino Espirito Santo*—
Divine Holy Spirit.

On the knoll at the south corner of Taylor Street stood the old
Methodist Meetinghouse known affectionately as "The Old Sloop"
until George Rogers moved it to Bass Rocks for his barn. The third
house on the left beyond Taylor, as Prospect descends back toward
the harbor, was the home of the late Captain Solomon Jacobs, "King
of the Mackerel Killers." Skipper Sol, they claimed, could smell a school
of mackerel beneath his keel. He roamed the world for new fishing
grounds, always led the fleet, and was a daring innovator of vessel
design and methods. Jacobs came from Newfoundland; he was typi-

cal of the "herring-chokers" and Bluenose Nova Scotians whose domination of the Gloucester sailing fleet by their sheer seamanship gave rise to much friendly joshing by the natives they fished with. The late sailmaker Albert Everett Flygare, whose own father was a skipper, told one story:

"It was an election eve before the First War, and the parties were having the usual torchlight parades, with the fishermen in their oilskins holding aloft the torches and banners. Down by the barroom at the corner of Elm and Main there was a wagon pulled up, with the candidate aboard, and Sol Jacobs with him, as Sol was very political-minded. And a big guy yells up from the crowd:

" 'Hey Jacobs, what the hell are you doin' up there? When you came down here to Gloucester you was so dumb you was peelin' doughnuts, you thought they was potatoes!'

" 'Yer dam right,' Sol roars back, and he reaches that big ham of a hand in his pocket and pulls out a fistful of bills would choke a halibut and waves them at the guy. 'And dam ye, here's the peelin's!' "

Upper Main Street

Prospect Street hooks into Main Street at Flannagan Square. This is Union Hill, and from the foot of it west to Pleasant Street over a century ago was Spring Street, of which a mere block remains, above Main Street. Halfway down Union Hill on the south side of Main Street was the Dewey Theater (for the victorious admiral of the Battle of Manila at the height of the Spanish-American War of 1898), an intimate bistro of burlesque on the street floor of the Landrys' rooming house. The Landry kids bored holes through the flooring above the stage, and their pals took turns peeping at the show. On the upland side of the street are several old houses of distinct character. Farther down, just below Gorton's newer office building, was the famous Union Hill Theater. It could pack in 1,300 seventy years ago and did, and it boasted the biggest stage north of Boston, so big that the horse race in *Country Fair* was run with real live horses trotting across it on a treadmill.

In the next block on the left stands the sturdy brick Blackburn Building, identified across the second story, built in 1900 by Gloucester's all-time fisherman-sailor hero, Howard Blackburn, for his saloon and home (map 8, 3). The giant Nova Scotian rowed sixty miles into Newfoundland with the frozen body of his dorymate, five days without

38. *Howard Blackburn at the wheel of his last sloop,* Cruising Club, *in 1929. The Lone Voyager is seventy.*

food or water, after they were separated in a gale from the Gloucester schooner *Grace L. Fears* in the winter of 1883. Blackburn survived but lost all his fingers by frostbite; he returned to Gloucester to keep a saloon, now the Halibut Point restaurant. In 1899 he sailed the sloop *Great Western* singlehanded, in spite of his disability, from Gloucester to England. The next year he built this building, and the next, in 1901, he repeated his astounding feat in the twenty-five-foot sloop *Great Republic*, this time to Portugal. That valiant craft was returned home after many more owners and voyages, has been restored by the Gloucester Historical Commission, and awaits the funds to enshrine it on the waterfront.

The collective memory of Howard Blackburn is reinforced annually by the international dory races between the young stalwarts of Gloucester and of the Lone Voyager's native Nova Scotia in mid-June and by the Blackburn Challenge Rowing Race of twenty-one miles around Cape Ann in late July.

The North Shore Theater next to Blackburn's was built on the vacant lot where carnivals once pitched their tents. Next on was the Hotel Savoy, dear to the Rotarian and the traveling man, sacrificed to urban renewal. And in the A&P parking lot was the glittering Olympia

Theater, movies spiced with three vaudeville acts daily and four on Friday, ''Bargain Day.'' How the fire whistle on top of the powerhouse, since silenced, tore the torpor from the love scenes of the silver screen on Main Street, shaking the very walls!

39. *Main Street in the 1880s, looking west, featured horsecars, cobblestones, and store awnings. Past Brown's store on the right at Pleasant Street was Wetherell's drugstore, now Birch; Gray's hardware was at the corner of Hancock Street, beyond on the left.*

At Fishermen's Corner, Main and Duncan, the men gathered to loaf and smoke and watch the passing scene and talk fishing, ''holding up the bank,'' or leaning against it anyway, waiting maybe for a site mackereling to the Bay Shore (Bay of St. Lawrence, that is), or fresh halibuting up to the Grand Banks, or off to Georges on a quick winter haddocking trip. Half down Duncan Street on the left was the venerable snug harbor of Gloucester, the Fishermen's Institute, started in 1891 as a bethel and home ashore when the waterfront was swarming with transient fishermen with all their loneliness and troubles. Left in the backwash, the old Institute and adjoining police station/courthouse succumbed to urban renewal and the demands of order and justice in the mid-1970s.

On the opposite corner occupied by the Birch drugstore were the rooms for years of the Master Mariners Association over Wetherell's

40. *Gloucester's first horsecar—destination Eastern Point—is dedicated in 1885 at Post Office Square, looking toward the head of Duncan Street and Fishermen's Corner from Pleasant.*

41. *The brick Post Office and Customs House, looking north up Pleasant Street, survived the fire of 1864. Since the 1960s the site of the Baptist Church has been a city parking lot.*

drugstore until it burned in 1946. This was the captains' club, founded in 1886, with two hundred members at its peak. That robust writer of the sea, James B. Connolly, was privy to their councils here and wrote of them around 1940 in *The Port of Gloucester:*

''In the Master Mariners' quarters, retired skippers nowadays heave themselves into wide chairs, fill a pipe or light a cigar, and observe the folk coming and going in the street.... The brothers of the sea not sitting out a watch at the big window will be at cards—at bridge, forty-five, or rummy. No betting is allowed in the room—nor liquor; but the interest in cards never lags. Men who have coolly measured an oncoming masthead sea in their day, perhaps spat contemptuously after one in passing, grow vastly excited here at times over a debatable point in a card game."

After the 1946 fire they moved to 119 Main Street upstairs, the master mariners fading away, then the club itself in 1971. The last of the grand old men, Captain Morton Selig, who had taken the schooner *Elsie* dory-trawling sixty-five years earlier, died at a vigorous one hundred in 1988.

4? *Howard Wheeler sold men's clothing—pure, simple, and very uncomfortable-looking for the average fisherman—next door to the Cape Ann Savings Bank on Main Street in 1880.*

Here at Fishermen's Corner is where Salem's steam pumper, rushed down on a flatcar, helped stop the great fire of the bitter night of February 18, 1864—that and blowing up Captain Fred Low's mansion at the east head of Duncan Street. The firemen and soldiers from the Eastern Point fort saved the brick Customs House across from it, later the site of Woolworth's (which, alas, left town in 1971) and now of the Senior Center, but that was about all. The fire started in Andrew Elwell's tailor shop at the rear of the block two hundred and fifty yards upwind on the east side of Porter Street. The northwest gale whipped it up the street through the frame buildings, jumped it across, and carried the sparks to the wharves. Herculean firefighting, bucket brigades, hand pumpers (the water froze in the pumps and they poured in liquor from the dramshops for antifreeze), explosives, the Salem steamer, and perhaps more luck than anything saved the rest of the town. At dawn

43. East on Main Street from below the Belmont Hotel at number 151, some time between the horsecars' arrival in 1885 and their surrender to the electrics in 1890.

44. After the Great Fire of February 18, 1864, looking east from the north side of Front (now Main) Street. The brick Post Office and Customs House at upper left survived; a hundred and three other structures didn't.

a hundred and three buildings lay in smoking ruins, thirty-eight families were homeless and fifteen acres of real estate were wiped out.

In the course of rebuilding, Front, Spring, Union Hill, and Jackson streets were integrated as Main Street. Rogers Street was created (named for merchant/promoter George H. Rogers) between Main and the new waterfront from Porter Street, where the fire started, to Water Street, where it stopped.

The West End

This second great fire finished the job begun by the first one of 1830. That blaze ignited in the early morning of September 16 behind Samuel Gilbert's house (where the liquor store stands) above the town landing. It moved along Front (Main) Street through the tinderlike wooden structures on the water side and down to the wharves as far as Porter Street, meanwhile jumping across at Short Street and consuming several buildings before it was halted by blasting.

Seventeen houses and forty-three stores and other places were destroyed—more than half of the business district and practically the whole of the West End, most of it uninsured. The fishermen were at sea, and the local militia was off on drill. Before help arrived from nearby towns, the volunteers were reinforced by three hundred Gloucester women who "with uncommon spirit" evacuated goods and furniture and kept a bucket brigade going for nearly eight straight hours—and by a party of Penobscot Indians who happened to be in town and who "exerted themselves with great bravery."

These two fires, less than thirty-four years apart, leveled most of the business and commercial heart of Gloucester, including many fine homes. Hardly had the town begun to recover from the blow of the first fire when it was struck by the Panic of 1837 and the depression that followed. The extent of the permanent setback that Gloucester suffered by these events has never been fully appreciated.

The most striking architectural result of the 1830 fire was the cooperative replacement of the classic colonial frame homes, whose gardens looked out on the harbor, with brick structures in the Federalist style forming at least three continuous street fronts. Two of these on the south side of Main Street, along with a couple on the north side, remain today.

*45. The west end of Front (Main) Street
after the blizzard of April 3, 1861, in one of the
earliest surviving photographs of Gloucester.*

The brick Babson Block was acquired by the late Roger W. Babson in part to contain his Isabel Babson Memorial Library for expectant mothers (the homesite of his seventeenth-century midwife ancestor). It curves west from the parking lot where for many years stood the old Strand Theatre, whose sociable rats occasionally joined the audience for the show. Sixteen years ago Harold Bell purchased the deteriorating block, with its intimate doorways and intriguing roof angles, and saved it from destruction; the city added the widened sidewalks and old-fashioned street lamps.

The next block beyond is anchored on the west corner of Boynton's Alley by the unusual stone structure quarried from what was at the time a nearby pasture behind Granite Street by the old Gloucester Bank, one of the new nation's first when organized in 1796 (map 8, 4). This was the first home of the Cape Ann Savings Bank from 1846 until that institution moved up street around 1892 to its present building at 109.

Alfred Mansfield Brooks in *Gloucester Recollected* told a good story about the old stone bank and its president, John Somes, former Gloucester sea captain and Revolutionary privateersman, who was seated at a table one day signing banknotes when a man with a pistol burst in and growled, "This is the end of your usury, old Shylock!"

"Not by a damn sight!" roared the banker, leaping up, and floored him. When the treasurer came into the room, Captain Somes was still coolly signing notes, and without looking up, ordered: "Call the constable and have the damned corpse taken away. The directors will be here in a few minutes."

The "corpse" was unconscious merely. And his intended victim was sitting on the trap door in the floor that was the only access to the bank's underground stone vault.

The bank's new quarters at 109 Main Street is another tour de force of the ubiquitous George H. Rogers. After the 1864 fire Rogers bought the granite building of the City Bank on State Street in Boston, dismantled it, brought it to Gloucester in one of his vessels, and reassembled it, stone by stone, on this spot.

The northwest end of Main Street is moored to the splendidly restored brick structure that escaped the 1830 fire, known variously since 1810 as the Atlantic House, the Gloucester House, Tappan's Folly (after builder James Tappan), the Puritan House, the Mason House, the Gloucester Hotel, and the Community House. The brick block with granite posts and lintels was built after that fire, as were the 1831 bricks west of the St. Peter's Club of the Sicilian-American fishing community. But the first of those, the once elegant Mansfield town house of a dozen fireplaces, curving stairways with mahogany railings, recessed window seats, marble mantels, and black walnut floors, was torn down for the filling station.

Where else in Gloucester can we peel back the layers of our history and find such a succession of life styles, such proliferation of paradox?

Middle Street

Middle Street is less stratified but much more nearly a museum row because it was to windward of the two great fires, and because its one-block distance and the loyalty of generations of property owners have held commercial exploitation in some reasonable check. It hasn't remained inviolate, yet in the face of creeping tastelessness more than a dozen of the handsome homes that the well-to-do shipowners and captains built before the Revolution on this rather intimate height above the waterfront still grace the street in varying states of preservation, with two historic churches and a few delightful oddities.

So let's start from the harbor end of Western Avenue, noting in passing the pair of gambrels at Riggs Street, and above them at 20 Middle the pleasing colonial mansion built in 1770 by Captain John Somes.

The narrow, aristocratic brick at the corner of Angle Street (map 8, 5) was the home of Gloucester's late historian and connoisseur, Swarthmore College Professor Alfred Mansfield Brooks, and is literally pedigreed. It was put here about 1850 by that inveterate mover and shaker, George Rogers. He bought in Boston the interior of an 1820 Charles Street house and a 1790 West Cedar Street house attributed to Charles Bulfinch, barged them down to Gloucester as was his wont, placed the Bulfinch atop the 1820, and built the brick shell around the two. Think of it—mahogany doors with silver hinge plates....

At Legion Square is the classic Town Hall of 1844, which served until its short-lived successor was dedicated on Dale Avenue in 1867. With columns on two sides, it's one of the few remaining examples of the Greek Revival of the 1840s. When the town moved out, the Forbes School moved in, and then after World War I the building was leased to the American Legion.

The equestrian Joan of Arc incongruously leading the charge up the Legion steps is the creation of the internationally known sculptress Anna Vaughn Hyatt Huntington, daughter of the Annisquam marine scientist Alpheas Hyatt. How the Maid of Orleans came to be on top of the World War I memorial may be inferred from the fact that its creator was undoubtedly a friend of Eastern Point resident A. Piatt Andrew, a founder of the American Field Service, which had young Americans driving ambulances at the front in France before their country entered the war; Andrew was a neighbor of artist Frederick Hall, who designed the base, and a founder of the American Legion, to whose Gloucester post, it is said, the French government presented Saint Joan.

The model for the steed was an East Gloucester fire station horse, a far cry from France, where Joan's inspiring life and martyrdom "haunted the artist with an insufferable fascination," according to the sculptress's biographer. The original statue was erected on New York's Riverside Drive in 1915, just before America entered World War I, and won her the Purple Rosette of the French government. For a replica sent to Boise, France, in 1921 she was made a Chevalier of the Legion of Honor. Other replicas went to San Francisco, to Quebec City's Plains of Abraham—and to Washington Street in Gloucester, Massachusetts, her summer home.

Long before Saint Joan conquered Town House Square it was the scene of Gloucester's annual display of Fourth of July fireworks, an all-too-explosive mixture of powder and rum that was abruptly terminated, according to Alfred Mansfield Brooks, when a stray spark one year lit in the chest containing the arsenal. The rockets went off all at once, causing a stampede, and people were hurt but no one killed. Now the city puts on a harbor spectacular from Stage Fort Park for the Fourth, and those who are not in it turn out to watch the parade of the year, the Antiques and Horribles—Horribles for short—of long tradition.

On the south corner of Washington and Middle streets is the house built around 1760 by Samuel Whittemore, excellently restored for apartments. A block along Middle on the same side is number 43, built by William Stevens about the same time, and across the street number 44, where a pair of seashells three feet from rim to rim flanked the pleasant old dooryard many years ago. The house then was occupied by the Stacy sisters, Fannie and Mary, and their brother, dapper Jim, who ran a Main Street haberdashery, cousins of the writer, and all unmarried. The ell at the rear was a "dame school" for the genteel children of Gloucester, opened by Miss Mary in the 1870s on the urging of a mother who found the language and manners to which the fishermen's children subjected her darling in the public school too horrible to be tolerated.

Among the city's most happily designed public buildings is the Independent Christian Church (map 8, 6). Its shaded equanimity belies the storms of controversy that have never ceased to swirl around its lack of orthodoxy. This is the seat of Universalism in America, erected in 1805 and originally led by The Reverend John Murray, who imported, from England in 1779, the radical belief that all souls are to be saved. The bell in the restored and dramatically illuminated steeple was cast by Paul Revere in 1806, the date of the Willard clock on the balcony. The fine whale oil chandelier of Sandwich glass was hung in 1823.

Soon after the Gloucester Universalists organized under Mr. Murray, the town tried to drive him out and confiscate the congregation's property in reprisal for their refusal to pay taxes for the support of the First Parish, the established church from which they had defected. Arguing that freedom of religion and its compulsory support are incompatible, they sued to recover under the Bill of Rights of the new Massachusetts Constitution that guaranteed separation of church and state, and won their case in the historic decision of 1786.

The Sargent-Murray-Gilman-Hough House (map 8, 7) at 49 Middle Street, a superb example of colonial Georgian architecture, lords it over Main Street below. It was built probably in 1781–83 by Winthrop Sargent, a leading merchant, ardent patriot, and early adherent of Universalism, for his daughter Judith. After her first husband, John Stevens, left her (and the country) she married Preacher Murray, and this was the home hearth of Universalism while they remained in Gloucester. It came into the Gilman family, and The Reverend Samuel Gilman, the author of "Fair Harvard," was born here. For some forty years the house was owned by Benjamin K. Hough, treasurer of the church.

In 1915 this house was in danger of demolition. The Universalist General Convention and the Sargent family raised restoration funds. Its former frontage on Main Street was acquired and cleared, and the original terraces and gardens were recreated. Much Americana has been donated for furnishings, including works by Fitz Hugh Lane and paintings, sketches, and memorabilia of the family's artistic genius, John Singer Sargent. It is open to the public June through September.

Across the cozy courtyard at 51 Middle Street is the home built about 1752 by Samuel Chandler, pastor of the First Parish Church and author of the most revealing diary of Gloucester's colonial period. Number 57, beyond, was probably erected in the same period by James Hayes.

Across at 58 Middle Street is the birthplace of Roger Babson and the former home of the Open Church Foundation that he founded in 1942 to encourage churches to remain unlocked as sanctuaries for meditation. It was built by Daniel Rogers, an ancestor of the writer, before the Revolution. Next on at 64 is the Rogers-Warner-Haskell house, circa 1752, then at 70 the Ezekiel Woodward house, built about 1756.

In the next block we come to Temple Ahavath Achim (Temple of

46. The Sawyer Free Library in its early days of a century ago was freer vertically than horizontally.

Brotherly Love), formerly the Unitarian Church (map 8, 8), built in 1828 as the clouds of another local schism gathered, on the site of the demolished First Parish Meetinghouse that had stood here since 1738. For generations there hung proudly in the entry a cannonball fired by the enraged Captain Lindsay from his British sloop-of-war *Falcon* that August day of 1775. So frustrated was Lindsay by the Gloucester patriots in his efforts to regain a prize he had chased into the harbor (losing three dozen captured and killed in the process) that from one until five in the afternoon he cannonaded the town, venting his special wrath on the church whose bell had been ceaselessly pealing the alarm. "Now my boys," tradition says he shouted to his men, "we will aim at the damned Presbyterian Church! One shot more, and the house of God will fall before you!" Not Presbyterian, of course, but at that time Congregational.

Hard against what is now the temple property line and only twelve feet from the west wall of his house, which was later bought by Samuel Sawyer for the library, John Beach around 1800 built a ropewalk the entire seven hundred fifty feet of the block from Middle to Prospect streets. Fully a hundred and twenty-five feet longer than the more conspicuous one above Pavilion Beach, it was tailored to the twisting of anchor cable for Gloucester vessels, a standard a hundred and twenty fathoms, or seven hundred and twenty feet. But by the 1850s only the harbor ropewalk remained.

The Sawyer Free Library (map 8, 9) is privately owned, although it serves the city and is operated largely with public funds. It started as the Gloucester Lyceum, a lecture group launched in 1830 whose library was largely destroyed in the 1864 fire. Seven years later Samuel Sawyer gave the Lyceum $10,000 and his name. The lectures gave way to books, and in 1884 Sawyer donated this house, built by Thomas Sanders in 1764 (the eccentric Englishman John Beach having in the meanwhile piled on two bizarre-appearing stories), as a library building. The Sawyer today has a fine collection of Cape Ann literature and a modern building erected in 1976.

47. *Middle Street of a bygone day, from the lawn of the Unitarian Church. The site of Dr. Ebenezer Dale's graceful colonial home and Captain Solomon Davis's "Temple" is now occupied by the YMCA. The Joseph Foster house on the far corner of Hancock Street (with the store front) has been preserved and restored.*

Dale Avenue was named for Dr. Ebenezer Dale, who died in 1834. The physician's house, on the site of the town whipping post, was moved to Grove Street to make room in 1904 for the YMCA. In 1965 the Y razed "Solomon's Temple," a handsome, colonnaded Greek Revival house to its immediate west built by Solomon H. Davis about 1840, and replaced it in 1973 with the present enlarged brick structure.

Beyond the library on Dale Avenue, the corridors of the former Central Grammar School no longer ring with the shouts of generations but reflect the measured tread of the senior occupants of Central Grammar Apartments, a nationally recognized pioneer conversion of its type. The school was phased out in 1971 with the acquisition by the city of the St. Peter's Catholic High (now Fuller) School at Blackburn Circle. From 1889 until its replacement rose from the city dump in 1939 Central had been Gloucester's High School; its predecessor, on Mason Street, was built in 1850 and burned in 1887.

Across Dale Avenue, Gloucester's new town hall of 1867 served but two years before it burned to a shell on May 16, 1869. The worst loss was a panoramic painting of the town, some said his best, by Fitz Hugh Lane. Today's multitowered National Historic Site is more imposing than the original (map 8, 10), dedicated on June 22, 1871, two years before the town turned city. Long before they built the Union Hill Theater in 1900, ship chandler Frank W. Lothrop and grocer James E. Tolman produced theatricals in the since-restored City Hall auditorium, which has resounded to dances, plays, concerts, vaudeville and musical comedy, wrestling, boxing, basketball, and about every other diversion imaginable—not to mention the continuing political drama— in an old fishing port that knows wild times. The restored tower is a hundred and forty-eight feet above the street and a hundred and ninety-four above sea level. The clock was given by Samuel Sawyer. If you climb the tower, the circular windows at the very pinnacle will reward you with bird's-eye views of the city guaranteed to take away what breath you have left.

The granite wall along Dale Avenue and Warren Street was put together by the WPA during the Depression of the 1930s, as was the granite Post Office adjoining City Hall.

The northeast corner of Middle Street and Dale Avenue has been occupied since 1765 by the Hardy-Parsons house (map 8, 11), owned by the Cape Ann Historical Association though not open to the public; the sunken garden at the rear is dedicated to the memory of Alfred Mansfield Brooks, the Historical's late president.

The southeast corner of Middle and Hancock streets belongs to the house of the same vintage occupied by Colonel Joseph Foster (map 8, 12), a local leader in the Revolution. It was restored in 1972 by the Cape Ann Bank and Trust Company, now the Bank of New England.

The Foster House is in a vulnerable spot. On the morning of September 26, 1913, the fire department had assembled on Prospect Street and was thundering one piece after another down Dale Avenue and wheeling to the right into Middle Street for a motion picture being filmed by the Gloucester Theater. Chief Crowe's car, the auto chemical, the steamer going for all it was worth, and the hose carriage had careened around the corner, which was packed with vehicles and spectators, when the hook and ladder came clattering along with eight firemen aboard.

Well, the driver lost control. They couldn't make the corner, and the momentum of the rig drove the two handsome horses right through the windows of Boardman's piano and sewing machine store on the street floor of the Foster House and catapulted the man at the reins in on top of them, badly hurt. The other firemen and the spectators escaped, but the horses were so gashed by glass that the gutter flowed with blood, and one had to be shot. Eight years later a fellow taking a driving lesson on Dale Avenue became so flustered by his instructor's directions whether to turn right or left that he did neither, and again Boardman's windows were shattered.

Pleasant Street

The fanciest brickwork in Gloucester adorns the Albert Garland house at the corner of Middle and Pleasant streets. Note the rococo dormer on Pleasant: the flue from the fireplace below divides around the window and reunites itself at the chimney!

Nearly across Pleasant Street is another pleasing specimen of the neoclassic revival of the 1840s, built by Captain Harvey Coffin Mackay in 1842, formerly the home of the writer's grandparents.

Next north is the building of the Cape Ann Scientific, Literary and Historical Association (its full name) (map 8, 13), founded in 1873 as another outgrowth of the Lyceum from which the Sawyer Free Library sprang. Jacob Smith—he who designed and erected the Independent Christian Church—built the Historical's present house for Captain Elias Davis, Sr., in 1804. (The nearly matching private house across Federal Street arose simultaneously.) The Davis house was acquired in 1923 with funds given long since by Addison Gilbert. The attached museum and hall at the back were built in 1936 from the bequests of Lucy Browne

Davis and her sister Catalina. The "wing" on the site of the old Salvation Army headquarters was given anonymously in 1969. The brick building behind the museum on Elm Street, formerly occupied by the National Marine Fisheries Service (now headquartered in Blackburn Industrial Park) and before that by the telephone company, was purchased by the Historical in 1989 to expand its facilities.

At the heart of the Cape Ann Historical Association's collections are more than thirty-five paintings and a hundred drawings and lithographs by Gloucester's and America's great luminist marine artist, Fitz Hugh Lane (1804–65). Here, appropriately, is by far the largest gallery anywhere of the artist's glowing recreation of the Gloucester and Maine coast of the mid-nineteenth century.

Here, too, is the silver communion service of the First Parish, made by Paul Revere. The marine room displays a fleet of rare and handsome models of Gloucester vessels along with artifacts, art, and graphic displays relating to the fisheries. The archives of Cape Ann literature, periodicals, manuscripts, maps, charts, logs, early records, and illustrative materials are scholarly and accessible. Room after room of the Davis house is stocked with period furnishings and the profusion of articles brought back by Gloucester's far-sailing seafarers in its days of world trade. And finally, there is the dory Centennial, which the young Gloucester fisherman Alfred Johnson sailed on a dare to England in 1876, the first singlehanded crossing of the Atlantic on record. "Centennial" Johnson returned to Gloucester a hero, although years after he'd retired from the sea as one of Gorton-Pew's skippers, he admitted that he was a "damn fool" to try it.

Here by this famous old dory, the symbol of all that is daring and dauntless in the spirit of Gloucester, we conclude our downtown tour with a pondering of the past upon which the future would best be built.

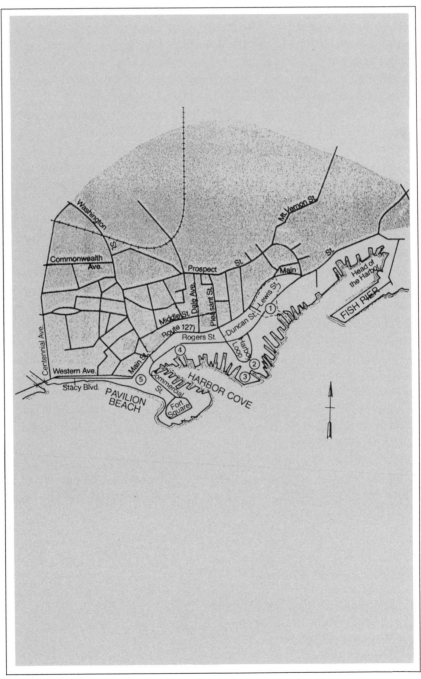

Map 9. The Waterfront

CHAPTER 9

THE WATERFRONT

*We lived on Kent Circle next door to Captain Charlie Harty, and I
spent many hours watching the big schooners go out under tow with
the tug* Eveleth. *I can still hear the blocks creak as the mains'l was
hoisted. When we had an easterly storm I was sure the schooners
would run ashore in front of us as they tacked in past Ten Pound
Island with the mains'l booming like thunder when they came about
on the other tack.*

—Letter from a Gloucester native in Michigan

This oldest fishing port in the western hemisphere still plies its
trade with courage and resourcefulness, but two immense
challenges put the city's fiber sorely to the test as it launched
into its fourth century. The first was the shift from sail to power that
displaced almost without a trace not only a fishing technology but a
way of life, indeed a unique society. By that fateful day in 1927 when
the fabled schooner *Columbia* embarked on Gloucester's final saltfish-
ing trip under sail, everyone knew that the days, the hours, of canvas
were numbered.

By the 1930s the fleet that had peaked at more than four hundred
schooners, and the major part of the old shore establishment that built
and served those noble vessels, were all but gone. The skills of generations were of little use to anyone any more. Sail was through. So were
dory trawling, handlining, and jigging as pursuits of any major con-
sequence, and the bait and salt industries, the acres of flake yards, the
smokehouses, the blacksmith shops, the spar yards and sail lofts. The
diesel engine and the otter trawl, the draggers, had taken over.

Still the waterfront, for all this upheaval, clung to the threadbare
look of yesteryear. Proud schooners had their tall spars and spiking

bowsprits cropped, their bulkheads cut for engines, and their bilges mucked with fuel oil so they could go dragging. The acrimonious International Fishermen's Races with Canada were a glorious, growling last gasp, a funeral feast for a Viking about to be buried at sea in the bosom of his craft.

And then came quick-freeze, the second half of the punch, the revolution in refrigeration that took away most of Gloucester's advantage in marketing fresh fish. It enabled any nation in the world with the technology to fish anywhere in the world, and to sell anywhere, by means of mechanical refrigeration. Gloucester's traditional fishing grounds thus were invaded by foreign factory fleets, and the very fish taken from its backyard were delivered to its front door by the refrigerated freighters, the "reefers," of the competition.

The adoption of the two hundred-mile limit in 1977 following the Law of the Seas Conference cleared our offshore banks of the foreign fleets and gave a short-lived spur to American fishermen. Younger men were attracted to fishing, although they had to borrow at the high interest rates then current to build new vessels.

The euphoria didn't last. High-technology fish-finding techniques, overfishing, the division of Georges Bank by treaty, giving the richer portion to Canada in the mid-1980s, diminishing stocks, the inability of the fishermen to work collectively, environmental pollution, competition from Canadian imports, escalating waterfront land values, even insurance-scuttling, all took their toll. By 1989 Gloucester's dwindling fleet was a poor relation in its own front yard.

Today, few traces of the old waterfront remain.

The Fish Pier

From the end of Route 128, Parker Street takes us to the State Fish Pier past new wharves, fishing and commercial property built under the aegis of the Gloucester Redevelopment Authority on waterfront cleared under urban renewal. Ninety years ago on the right, at the Head of the Harbor, was the large shop and boatyard of Higgins & Gifford, the most prolific builders of small craft in our history, among them Centennial Johnson's dory and two or three other cockleshells that crossed the Atlantic in like foolhardy but watertight fashion. The partners specialized in seineboats, dories, surfboats, whaleboats, and small

48. *From the Parker Street hill above the Head of the Harbor and Smoky Point. In this 1920s view, Five Pound Island, Duncan's Point beyond it, and Rocky Neck at left evoke Fitz Hugh Lane's perspective of seventy years earlier (on the cover).*

yachts, and boasted in 1875 that if put bow to stern all the craft they had produced in their first four years alone would stretch two and a half miles. By 1892 they had turned out 3,500 and were just getting their second wind.

The entrance to the Fish Pier marks where until fifty-two years ago Smoky Point (for the number of establishments that smoked halibut and herring, principally) stopped and the harbor began. After great debate, the state put up $660,000, the federal Public Works Administration $540,000, and the city $100,000 (including $12,000 for Five Pound Island), and the project of building a fish pier from Smoky Point to the island to match Boston's was embarked on in the Depression year of 1937. Completed eighteen months later, on September 15, 1938, the project included the freezer, ice-making plants, and stalls for processors.

Conceived in political controversy, the State Fish Pier operated under intermittent clouds until it was turned over in 1982 to the Massachusetts Land Bank, which is spending $7 million to tear down the obsolete structures and build new wharves for the fleet. The old plant for rendering trash fish and gurry into dehydrated protein—the "De-Hyde"—is to be replaced, it's hoped, by a new, high-tech, low-odor rendering operation to take advantage not only of fish by-products but of large underutilized stocks of menhaden, herring, and mackerel.

Ample space will be available for lease to private owners to build modern processing plants, all on the assumption that there will be a cyclical resurgence of the fisheries, given effective resource management.

The star boarder at the Pier since August 27, 1988, when she sailed home to a tumultuous welcome in Gloucester, has been the a hundred and twenty-two-foot knockabout schooner *Adventure*, built by the James yard in next-door Essex in 1926 for Captain Jeff Thomas. She was the last American dory-trawler when she was retired from commercial fishing under Captain Leo Hynes in 1953 and sold for refit as a Maine passenger windjammer. *Adventure* was given by Captain Jim Sharp to The Gloucester Adventure, a nonprofit educational corporation, ''as a monument to the history of Gloucester and for the education and pleasure of the public.''

49. *The knockabout fishing schooner* Adventure, *built in Essex in 1926, heads out Gloucester Harbor past the Rockaway Hotel on Rocky Neck in the dim background. It's 1937, and she's off on a dory-trawling trip under Captain Leo Hynes.*

By walking clear to the end of the Fish Pier we reach the last dirt of Five Pound Island, where farther back than most of us can remember there were some fishing shacks and a wharf or two, and far previous to that probably five sheep pounds to half-match the ten on Ten Pound Island.

Out there between the spindle and the freezer piers to our right, long before the channel was dredged and when there wasn't water to float a deep-draft vessel at low tide, Captain Lindsay and the British *Falcon* on August 8, 1775 chased a Salem-bound West Indian schooner hard aground on the flats. The First Parish Church bell clanged forth the alarm. The patriots dropped everything and mustered around the shore. Lindsay sent thirty-seven men in boats to seize the prize. A smart skirmish followed, during which three Redcoats were killed.

The infuriated captain of the *Falcon* shelled the town and dispatched a boat around to the Fort beach to set the fish flakes afire and burn this hotbed of rebels to the ground, but our people rushed to the spot and captured them all.

In the meantime, out here before us, the Gloucestermen kept up their fire, and then they waded out, rescued the schooner, and took cutter, barges, and invaders. We lost two of our own, Peter Lurvey and Benjamin Rowe.

Captain Lindsay sailed out the beautiful harbor which spreads forth yonder and was never seen in these waters again.

Leaving the Fish Pier, we turn left on Main Street across from Dog Hill of forgotten pedigree and pause in the city park at the Head of the Harbor named in memory of Gordon W. Thomas, the leading modern chronicler of the old-time fishing fleet and the waterfront he loved, who picked *Adventure*'s name for Captain Jeff, his father. From this spot in 1847 Fitz Hugh Lane executed the painting on the cover of this book, looking across to Five Pound Island and on out the harbor *he* loved.

Everything from the Thomas Park to Rowe Square—once the wharves of Jordan, Perkins, Babson, and Sylvanus Smith and home to a hundred schooners—has been cleared out by urban renewal and replaced with modern fish taking-out and processing plants and vessel and yacht servicing facilities.

50. *Splitting and salting a trip of fish from the schooner* Evelyn M. Thompson *at the Perkins wharf, later Gorton-Pew, below Rowe Square, April 19, 1912, according to Eben Parson's photo log.*

51. *The 1,565-ton salt ship* Yallaroi, *built of iron in Aberdeen in 1855, dries her canvas at Pew's salt wharf, now Gorton's, on August 15, 1914. The steam lighter* Abbott Coffin *lies alongside.*

Going west from Rowe Square along much-widened Rogers Street are Gorton's sprawling Seafood Center and the Americold (formerly Quincy Market) freezers, sandwiching the standby generators of the Massachusetts Electric Company.

Not since the Surinam trade was at its richest in 1857, when ten barks and ten brigs arrived with cargoes worth $400,000 from South America, has Gloucester seen such foreign commerce, now ironically in millions of pounds of frozen fish blocks brought in by refrigerated freighters for processing into frozen dinners locally or in similar plants around the country.

The Ghost of Vincent's Cove

Gloucester claims three major ghosts among a legion of lesser ones: Dogtown Common, Five Pound Island, and Vincent's Cove. Of the last nary a trace, not a teaspoon of salt water, remains. Seventy-five years ago Vincent's Cove was here and very much alive; today its site would make a fascinating archeological dig, if dig we could through the middle of Rogers Street, under which somewhere are buried the bones, for instance, of Jimmy Brennan's and Charley McPhee's Friendship sloop.

The older charts show Vincent's Cove lined with wharves (map 9, 1). Before that it was Spring Cove for the brook that flowed in, earlier than that Ellery's for a man who owned part of it, and originally Vinson's after William Vinson, the settler who was granted this land and also Five Pound Island.

Where was it? Imagine the tide lapping at the curb of Main Street from the A&P parking lot east to beyond the Blackburn building! The entrance was between the end of the Electric Company property and Americold and only fifty yards wide. On the map it looked like a clenched and cocked left fist, the wrist making the narrows. Then in the 1870s the length of the dock parallel with Main Street was filled in to a width of around a hundred and twenty-five feet. So it remained until the time of World War I, when the abutters resumed dumping around the edge of the flats; they were joined by the city, and soon, as these things go, Vincent's Cove was a memory.

One who remembered it vividly was Charles McPhee, a veteran seaman who grew up in his grandmother Joanna Prior's boardinghouse at 301 Main Street, next east to Howard Blackburn's. Charley was a wharf rat then, running errands for Captain Blackburn and every morning, first thing, rowing the dory across Vincent's Cove after wood for his grandmother's stove.

So let's step aboard and oar with boatman McPhee in retrospect around his ghost cove, commencing clockwise at the east pier of the Americold freezer. Americold marks the west side of the entrance to the cove, built on the site of "Burkey's," the wharf of the later mayor John Burke—ex–Sherman Ruth's—ex–the final wharf of the Boston and Gloucester Steamboat Company—ex–the New England Fresh Fish Company's—Ex–Low's Wharf—ex–Pearce's in the Surinam and West

52. *The summer excursion steamer* Cape Ann *gets under way for Boston around 1912 after an assist from the steam tug* Nellie *at right. Beyond* Nellie's *bow in this photograph by waterfront chronicler Ernest Blatchford is probably the gaff-rigged sloop* Wenham Lake, *which replenishes the freshwater supply of the schooners from its "well" below deck.*

Indies trade. How the summer excursionists streamed down the ramp of the regal white SS *Cape Ann*! And how the high-pitched blast of the ugly, sturdy old SS *City of Gloucester*'s steam whistle every thirty seconds echoed from shore to shore as she churned out the slip and throbbed through the harbor in the foggy predawn, bound for Boston with a cargo of fish! And the red flag stuck out the steamboat company's office window, signaling the nearest towboat to come in for orders. . . .

The shore of Vincent's Cove ran diagonally from the steamship wharf across Americold's truck lot and under the corner of the office to Lewis Street. Along here were a factory making isinglass from hake sounds, and Dodd's cod liver oil works.

Tom Irving's shipyard is buried under the parking lot at the northeast corner of Rogers and Lewis streets; his dock penetrated almost halfway up the block toward Main Street, so his vessels slid into the cove where Rogers Street is. Irving was a master shipwright and also one of the finest makers of builder's models of schooners anywhere; examples are on display at the Cape Ann Historical Museum and the Smithsonian Institution in Washington.

53. *As dependable as she was ugly, the SS* City of Gloucester *plowed back and forth to Boston all year long with fish, freight, and folks from 1883 until 1925.*

Now we row with Charley across the parking lots of the old North Shore Theater and Gorton's, visualizing the backlot outhouses of Blackburn and Granny Prior and some long-gone Main Street establishments such as Nelson's oilskin plant, at the northeast end of the cove; from here Skipper McPhee leans on his port oar and rows us back across Rogers Street to John Bishop's shipyard about where the Electric Company's brick building is.

John Bishop and brother Hugh, who built Blackburn's sloop *Great Western* at his own yard at the head of Walen's wharf next to Burnham's railways on Duncan's Point, were ship carpenters. One of John's last was the pretty schooner *Stiletto*, launched in 1910. The cove was narrow at his ways, and he had to let his vessels in easy and brake them with heavy lines and drags from fetching up against the opposite wharf.

On the south side of Rogers Street, across from the theater parking lot, the towboats nudged in the barges from Norfolk, Virginia, alongside Friend's coal company wharf, 1,000 or 1,500 tons to a barge, and all hand-unloaded by a roving gang of coal lumpers at five cents per

54. *The fifty-four foot schooner* Actor *splashes from Tom Irving's shipyard into Vincent's Cove at the site of Gorton's lower parking lot. The Baptist Church and City Hall peek over the rooftops on this wintry day in 1902.*

man per ton, as Charley recalled it, pretty good pay eighty years ago for three days' work. We wind up our Stygian cruise with boatman McPhee, leaving Vincent's Cove on the east shore, rowing right through the Electric Company's bank of generators, drifting by the ghost schooners at the ghost pier of Sam Lane's fish company, and back to reality.

Rest in peace, Will Vinson's Cove, and all the life of it for three hundred years—buried.

Duncan's Point

West on Rogers Street past Americold the waterfront opens up to view again. This is Duncan's Point. Fitz Hugh Lane built the striking granite house of seven gables that dominates the knoll for his studio more than a year before Hawthorne's work of the same name was published in 1851 (map 9, 2). Some time after Lane's death it was used briefly for a jail, dubbed the "Old Stone Jug." Crowded almost out of sight by tenements for the next ninety years, this was the only home in the first urban renewal project preserved by the Gloucester Housing Authority, which has restored it for civic use and for the view that inspired the handicapped genius to put it all on canvas.

Lane built where a score of years before his birth Gloucester's patriots gathered one night around an ancient oak, twenty-three feet in circumference, to decorate it with lights and celebrate the end of their Revolution—"and, although no living person could remember the grandeur of its maturity," as Historian Babson wrote, "all agreed that it could not have surpassed the splendor which it now exhibited in its decay."

Embedded at the foot of the Lane house hill and park on the Rogers Street side is the granite doorstep of the First Baptist Church at Middle and Pleasant streets, which was torn down in 1966 and replaced by the modernistic structure with the "sail" east of Grant Circle. The step is eighteen by seven feet and a foot thick, and it took forty-two yoke of oxen to haul it from the quarry to the church some a hundred and fifteen years ago.

That clear-toned bell across from the new courthouse police station has been striking the hour and half-hour from the roof of the Gloucester Bank and Trust building, originally the Westerbeke Fishing Gear Company, only since 1972; it summoned the first eager pupils to the Sawyer School in 1869. Next door was the ship chandlery of L. D. Lothrop, inventor of the croaking pump foghorn no Gloucester schooner would sail past Eastern Point without.

Before urban renewal cleaned out Duncan's Point, what is now called Harbor Loop began here as the barroom end of "Drunken" Street, swung around the docks as Wharf Street from the little park, and returned to Rogers as Water Street, rimming the promontory settled in 1662 by Peter Duncan, a merchant of whom little is known except that the poor fellow was reported thirty years later to be impoverished and unable to work.

The Building Center is the successor to the Gloucester Coal Company, which is what Captain Charles T. Heberle called Bennett's wharf and coal pockets after he bought that firm out in 1903. Cap Heberle's early fame was in towboats that steamed about doing the harbor's close-quarters work—*Nellie, Priscilla, Charlie,* and *Mariner*—before auxiliary diesel engines in the schooners put them out of business. The one he built and held closest to his heart (she had steam steering and could turn on a nickel) was the *Eveleth*. At the end of Harbor Loop the small Solomon Jacobs Park honoring the King of the Mackerelers affords a close-up view of the harbor where the East Gloucester steam ferry used to land. The Gloucester Gas Light Company's wharf and gas works were here, and after the Boston steamers vacated it for Vincent's Cove, the towboats tied up along it for a while.

To our right the 1973 Coast Guard base (map 9, 3) is on the site of Parkhurst's marine railway, which hauled and patched and painted the fleet for more than a century before time caught up. Between the railway and Empire Fish was the enormous wharf of the Atlantic Halibut Company. Here hefty "Gloucestermen" like Captain Tommie Bohlin's fabled schooner *Nannie C. Bohlin* eased in from the banks—as she did, for instance, one September day in 1892 with 42,000 pounds of fresh halibut, every one of the four- or five-hundred pound monsters hauled aboard a dory by hand on a trawl line, sixteen days from dock to dock. Ten thousand tons of ice a year from Fernwood Lake cooled five million pounds of halibut shipped at the peak.

55. *Of the two schooners hauled up for work on Burnham's railways at Duncan's Point, the presence of a dory in her stern davits suggests the* Mabel Leighton *on the left is a "Georgesman" handlining on Georges Bank. After more than a hundred and forty years, the railway on the right continues in active service today here at the end of Harbor Loop.*

The Gloucester Marine Railway track, one of two built by the brothers Elias and Parker Burnham in 1849, must be among the oldest continually operating in the nation. Fitz Lane stationed himself on the Rocky Neck shore and sketched two vessels up on Burnham's, a schooner and George Rogers's three-masted Surinam "sugar wagon" *California*. The charges then were $10 for hauling and laying for one good working day—a "lay day"—and $5 a day for an extra day if under a hundred tons. The artist caught *California* just in time. Soon after, in 1857, she broke loose from the harbor in a January gale and swept across Boston Bay to her death on the rocks of Cohasset. The huge painting was a sign for a while over Burnham's paint shop and hangs today in the Cape Ann Historical.

Star Fisheries is on the former Walen wharf north of the railway. Next was Fabet Fisheries, razed by urban renewal, on the old John Chisholm wharf. E. L. Rowe's sail loft, one of the big ones in town and makers from scrap canvas of the Gloucester Bed Hammock, which swung on many a summer porch, was at the foot of the northeast slope under the Lane house, facing where the Americold freezer is. In the freezer parking lot were the two conical brick gas holders of the gas company. In the 1960s you'd have followed your ears to the old-time Independent and Gloucester machine shops, their storerooms piled with useless schooner hardware.

Beyond, on Leighton's wharf, was the last authentic sail loft in the city, Thomas's. Urban renewal wiped that out too. Charley Olsen, its

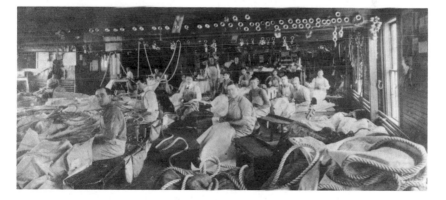

56. *Ben Colby's sail loft on Leighton's wharf had no shortage of work seventy-five years ago. Today the Americold freezer occupies the site.*

57. Timber tall and true awaits the call at Thurston's spar yard by the town landing at the head of Harbor Cove (today St. Peter's Park) about 1916. Shears at left hoist, lower, and step new masts in schooners. The hip roof of the Gilbert house at 1 Western Avenue is visible in the background.

president at the time, apprenticed in Ben Colby's loft there when he was sixteen at four dollars a week. In those days a row of sailmakers passed the heavy duck of a big schooner mainsail, stiff as boot leather, along their laps like corn on the cob, and the man or boy who couldn't hand-stitch ten yards an hour could start looking for another line of work.

Back on Rogers Street, the vacant lot west of the Building Center was held down by the strongest building in Gloucester, the reinforced concrete headquarters of the Frank E. Davis Company's world-famous mail order fish house. Frank E. was the smartest fish salesman in the business. "Back in 1885 they laughed at me—and now they call me a crank!" he exuberated in his 1936 catalog and recipe book. "I'm proud to be called a crank!" was his advertising slogan, and he boasted that over 200,000 families bought fish from him by mail. The future of this vacant lot, one of the last remaining windows on the harbor, hung in 1989 on the outcome of a public outcry against its proposed development as a shopping mall to be called Gloucester Landing.

Harbor Cove

Ambling on, we come to the Gloucester House restaurant and Seven Seas Wharf and inspect the fishing draggers and the men repairing

58. *The 1882 schooner*
Porter S. Roberts *lies
at the Cunningham
wharf on the Fort Point
shore of Harbor Cove.
Her crew abandoned
ship in a gale a few
years later; they took to
the dories and were
rescued, but the
Roberts was lost.*

gear. This is Harbor Cove, between Duncan's and Fort points, where the first settlers kept their boats and probably built some, such as the sixty-eight-foot vessel for which William Stevens in 1661 took part payment in "good muscovadoes [raw] Shugar, at 2d. by the pound at Barbados."

Across the dock, next to Captain Courageous restaurant, is the colorful Fisherman's Wharf (map 9, 4), in the 1930s the home of the Atlantic Supply Company and its fleet, managed by Ben Pine, whose racing schooners brought twilight fame to Gloucester. From the small park at the dock's edge we can almost picture the graceful and yet powerful sailing vessels that tied up at "Piney's Wharf," with their towering masts and nests of dories on deck, the reflections from the water dancing on their shining hulls, the last of which was the last all-sail fishing schooner built, the black and powerful *Gertrude L. Thebaud*.

From the year of her launch in Essex in 1930, the *Thebaud* was the game but smaller challenger in the series of races with Canada that began in 1920 with Gloucester's only capture of the International Fishermen's Cup by *Esperanto*. That rivalry culminated in the final match in

59. *Everything flying, the gallant fisherman-racer* Gertrude L. Thebaud *exemplified the power, beauty, and speed of the Gloucester schooner at its height—and on the eve of its demise—in the 1930s.*

1938 between the *Thebaud* and her arch-rival, Lunenburg's overpowering *Bluenose*, holder of the trophy since 1921.

Now *Adventure* represents and symbolizes them all, and the revived races off Eastern Point bring the great schooners of today together each Labor Day weekend for the most exciting tall ship sailing match of the year in Massachusetts Bay.

Long before Ben Pine had this wharf it was Boynton's, before that Central Wharf, before that the wharf of William Pearce and Sons a hundred and seventy years ago, when that firm and Winthrop Sargent's led Gloucester's brisk trade with Surinam on the north coast of South America. Pearce's barks and brigs docked here with sugar and molasses for his rum distillery up on Porter Street. Fishing was in a periodic slump, and the wharves were less redolent of salt codfish than of peppercorns and cocoa beans, grapes, figs, raisins and olives, lemons, wines, cotton bales and spices, coconuts, tamarinds, and plaintain. Pearce even sent from this wharf in 1833 the tall ship *Lewis* on a whaling voyage to keep his spermaceti works supplied. It was no great success; Gloucester had smaller fish to fry.

A century and a half passed, and Fishtown again went whaling—taking passengers this time to watch the humpbacks, finbacks, and minkes that congregate to feed on Stellwagen, or Middle, Bank, an hour's run in one of the large whalewatch boats operated by four fleets out of Gloucester between spring and fall. What an experience, observing and sometimes even petting these friendly, endangered, greatest mammals in existence!

60. *Martha Rogers Harvey caught the essence of Gloucester Harbor in the days of sail with her superb glass plate photographs of the 1890s. Ten Pound Island is at right, Eastern Point in the far background.*

Most of the fish firms in Harbor Cove seventy-five-odd years ago had glassed-in lookouts on their roofs. It was the job of the fastest rowers to watch for the fleet coming in around Eastern Point; then there'd be a dory race out the harbor to buy the first trip of fish. These emissaries were followed by the "streamers" who rowed around to returning schooners as they anchored in the stream, the channel, to buy up the spent rope, cook's grease, and such odds and ends of the trip. Others bought cod livers for Dodd's and Norwood's and the rest of the oil works. The "gaffers" hung around the schooners as they were being unloaded, gaffing into their dories the fish that were dropped overboard, for these strays were theirs by long custom.

Out of the traffic tangle at the west end of Rogers, Washington Street—the original way from Meetinghouse Green—leads straight through St. Peter's Park to the colonial public landing at the head of Harbor Cove. This spacious new plaza is the scene of Gloucester's renowned Fiesta. In 1926 some Sicilian fishermen enshrined a statue of their patron St. Peter. It was the beginning of the Fiesta the community has celebrated every year since, with Latin joyousness and religous devotion, on the weekend closest to June 29, the Feast Day of St. Peter. Fiesta is preceded appropriately by the New Fish Festival, promoting dishes featuring underutilized species in local restaurants, and culminates in the colorful blessing of the fleet off Pavilion Beach by a prelate of the Roman Catholic Church.

Here at St. Peter's Park is a good place for contemplating the changes three hundred and sixty-five years have wrought on the old port.

The southerly portion of the bricked parking lot here was George Thurston's spar yard seventy-five years ago, always a logjam of tall timber floating in the dock, waiting to be shaped into masts, booms, gaffs, and bowsprits for newly launched schooners hauled around by one of the towboats from the Essex shipyards for fitting out—or to replace a "stick" twelve or sixteen inches thick snapped to splinters in a gale of wind on Georges Bank.

The Fort

Fort Point and Rocky Neck are the gateway to Gloucester's protected Inner Harbor. The "Fort" was called Watch House Neck during the Revolution for earthwork thrown up on its height by the local patriots. The town ceded it to the United States in 1794; it was reactivated during the War of 1812 as Fort Defiance. Then it went to ruins and was brought back to life for the last time in the Civil War with two batteries of naval guns.

Walking down Commercial Street, we find on the right the Cape Ann Chamber of Commerce and its information center in the building of the former Cape Ann Manufacturing Company that parlayed fishermen's oilskins into the well-known sportswear label, Mighty Mac.

Cunningham and Thompson dominated the fisheries at the Fort, held out against the big four that coalesced into Gorton-Pew, and built the plant occupied until recently by O'Donnell-Usen fisheries on the right of Commercial Street above the beach about 1916. Then they succumbed, joined up, and failed, and the building was acquired in the 1920s by Clarence Birdseye. Here, with his Birds Eye Division of General Foods, he carried out the quick-freeze experiments that would revolutionize the food industry and Gloucester fishing. Here, on their wooden "flakes" above the beach, the men of Gloucester dried their catch for almost three hundred years before this plant put an end to salt fish. Here on this beach Captain Lindsay's men tried to set fire to those flakes—and the town—that day in August of 1775, and were captured by our minutemen before they could do either.

Counterclockwise around Fort Square we come to the former Cape Ann Fisheries wharf and plant, burned in 1970, where the casual weekend pollockers drop their hooks for the casual pollock. Forty million pounds of fresh fish went through this plant in 1943. Today nothing remains but the view.

From the high ground of the Fort we see how it commanded the harbor and still discern the earthwork on the steep side toward the city. Down the slope is 28 Fort Square, home of the late poet Charles Olson, a bear of a man six feet eight, bard of the beat generation, author of the "Maximus" poems, scholar, passionate lover of Gloucester, who died in 1970 at fifty-nine.

Here at the Fort the Sicilian community planted itself around 1895. Two or three fishermen were the first, by way of Boston. The Fort was all Irish then, and there was hell to pay. It remained hard going against resentment and prejudice, but the pioneers were joined by friends and families from Boston, while others arrived directly from the Sicilian fishing villages of Terrasini, Sciacca, Taormina, and others.

61. The Sicilian fishermen of Gloucester needed no marine railways early in the 1900s. To work on their colorful boats they careened them on Pavilion Beach—just as they had on the shores of the old country.

62. *Its famed arched porches distinguished the Pavilion Hotel in the 1870s as much by land as by sea.*

In the beginning the latest discoverers rowed their dories outside Eastern Point at dawn, baited their hooks and set their trawls, and returned before sunset, hauling their small craft up on Pavilion Beach. With early profits they acquired sloops and sailed to deeper waters. More fish, more profits, hard work, bigger boats, larger crews, more eager relatives and friends arriving, family boats, draggers, seiners, fleets of them, fish plants, oil dealerships, marine railways.

The uncertainty surrounding the future of the wharves and fishing establishments at the Fort that have for so long been at Gloucester's heart reflects the pressures on much of the waterfront for more profitable uses in the face of the industry's decline and the clamor of residential and tourist-oriented developers. The city has banned residential development along the Inner Harbor waterfront, and the Commonwealth of Massachusetts has decreed that only marine-related uses will be allowed. Environmentalists, of which Gloucester has a full share, are the fiercest watchdogs on Cape Ann.

Stacy Boulevard

Leaving the Fort, we follow Western Avenue to The Tavern (map 9, 5) on the harbor. This landmark was built by the late W. H. Smith in

1917 to replace the Surfside, which had burned three years earlier. The Surfside had originally been the Pavilion Hotel of breezily Victorian, double-tiered verandas and observation tower, caught on canvas in all its gingerbread by Fitz Hugh Lane when it was nearly the first sea-side resort hotel on the North Shore.

It occurred to Captain Ignatius Webber, retired from the sea, to build a "double-geered" windmill with "two run of stone" exactly here in 1814, to grind corn at the rate of twenty bushels an hour when the "vains" turned. One day in the winter of 1824 the wind backed around and blew down his "vains." The octagonal tower stood here overlooking the harbor until it was moved to a spot off Commercial Street to make way for the Pavilion in 1849. In 1877 the last remnant of Captain Webber's windmill was partially destroyed by fire and dismantled.

As early as 1817 there was a ropewalk here between Canal Street, as Western Avenue was then called, and the harbor. From the end of Stacy Boulevard at the public ramp beside The Tavern the building ran six hundred and twenty-five feet above the seawall, the longer the better for the men and boys trudging along twisting the hemp. Its west

63. *A southerly gale piles in to Pavilion Beach around 1910. The view is in line with 71 Western Avenue. Johnnie Morgan's sweet shop is astride today's mall, and Stacy Boulevard will run outside the seawall in another decade. The Man at the Wheel will stand sixty feet out in Gloucester Harbor from the post at the end of the wall.*

wall must have been about twenty feet beyond the Man at the Wheel. A shed where they tarred the finished cordage stood on the water side of the ropewalk, and across the road on the site of the Stage Fort apartments was Lem Gilbert's tan yard for curing sails. Years later, sections of the ropewalk were lopped off and rolled up to Lewis Court, so they say, for housing that is still there.

The half-mile of clean arc of Stacy Boulevard from The Tavern to Kent Circle along Gloucester Bay has struck travelers as rivalling the Via Caracciolo on the Bay of Naples, and as colorful when it's lined above the tide from one end to the other with the canopied booths of vendors offering their wares during the annual mid-August Gloucester Waterfront Festival. The esplanade was conceived by George Stacy when that flamboyant hotel man became park commissioner in 1908, brought to reality on the inspiration of the three hundredth anniversary celebration in 1923, and restored in 1988. To make way for it, Gloucester (which has always had a partiality for moving heavy things around) relocated up in the back streets the houses that crowded the harbor side of Western Avenue. Fill was dumped; a new seawall was made; trees were planted; the esplanade was laid out; the benches were bolted down; and three years before his death in 1928, Mr. Stacy saw his boulevard done, his promise kept.

They that Go Down to the Sea in Ships is all Leonard Craske's heroic Man at the Wheel needs for inscription. Stand here on the bastion of the boulevard, for the first time or the hundredth, and gaze up at this immense bronze figure of the Gloucester fisherman. He is braced against the cant of his schooner's deck, gripping her wheel, a weather eye on the set of his jib, shaping his course out this harbor, to come about out there beyond Eastern Point, sails thundering, spray flying across his bow, sheets hauled, full and by for the fishing banks.

Between the years of 1830 and 1897, a mere fraction of her saga on the sea, six hundred and sixty-eight of Gloucester's vessels never returned around the Point, nor 3,755 of her men.

Sang the psalmist:

They that go down to the sea in ships, that do business in great waters: These see the works of the Lord, and his wonders in the deep.

THE END

I ts literature is as varied and idiosyncratic as Gloucester itself and readily accessible at the Sawyer Free Library, including a microfilm record of an extraordinary run of daily and weekly newspapers over a span of a hundred and sixty years. On the other side of City Hall from the Library, the Cape Ann Historical Association has a rich complementary collection of archival material, periodicals, art, artifacts, prints, and photographs, and offers numerous show catalogs and publications of its own. All this and several new and secondhand book stores, print shops, and art galleries can be found around town for the collector.

General History

Babson, John J. *History of the Town of Gloucester*. 1860 (updated by J. E. G. 1972).
Brooks, Alfred M. *Gloucester Recollected: A Familiar History* (edited by J. E. G.). 1974.
Copeland, Melvin T , & Elliott C. Rogers. *The Saga of Cape Ann*. 1960.
Erkkila, Barbara H. *Hammers on Stone: The History of Cape Ann Granite*. 1980.
—— *Village at Lane's Cove*. 1989.
Garland, Joseph E. *Boston's North Shore: Being an Account of Life among the Noteworthy, Fashionable, Wealthy, Eccentric and Ordinary, 1823–1890*. 1978.
—— *Boston's Gold Coast: The North Shore, 1890–1929*. 1981.
—— *Eastern Point: A Nautical, Rustical, and Social Chronicle of Gloucester's Outer Shield and Inner Sanctum, 1606–1950*. 1971.
—— *Eastern Point Revisited: Then and Now, 1889–1989*. 1989.
—— *Guns off Gloucester*. 1975.
Hawes, Charles B. *Gloucester by Land and Sea*. 1923.
Kenny, Herbert A. *Cape Ann: Cape America*. 1971.
Mann, Charles E. *In the Heart of Cape Ann, or the Story of Dogtown*. 1906.
Pringle, James R. *History of the Town and City of Gloucester*. 1892.
Webber, William S., Jr. *Waterfront: Around the Wharves of Gloucester in the Last Days of Sail* (edited by J. E. G.). 1973.

Fisheries

Bartlett, Kim. *The Finest Kind: The Fishermen of Gloucester*. 1977.
Church, Albert C., & James B. Connolly. *American Fishermen*. 1940.
Garland, Joseph E. *Adventure: Queen of the Windjammers. Last of the Gloucester Fishing Schooners*. 1985.
—— *Down to the Sea: The Fishing Schooners of Gloucester*. 1983.
—— *Lone Voyager*. 1963. (The biography of Howard Blackburn.)
—— *That Great Pattillo*. 1966. (The biography of James W. Pattillo.)
McFarland, Raymond. *The Masts of Gloucester: Recollections of a Fisherman*. 1937.

Pierce, Wesley G. *Goin' Fishin': The Story of the Deep-Sea Fishermen of New England.* 1934.
Procter, George H. *The Fishermen's Memorial and Record Book.* 1873.
—— *The Fishermen's Own Book.* 1882.
Smith, Sylvanus. *Fisheries of Cape Ann.* 1915.
Story, Dana. *Frame-Up!: The Story of Essex, Its Shipyards and Its People.* 1964.
Testaverde, R. Salve. *Memoirs of a Gloucester Fisherman.* 1987.
Thomas, Gordon W. *Fast and Able: Life Stories of Great Gloucester Fishing Vessels.* 1973.
—— *Wharf and Fleet.* (Historic photographs.) 1977.

Guides

Along the Old Roads of Cape Ann. (by Susan Babson, *anon.*) 1923.
Chamberlain, Samuel, & Paul Hollister. *Beauport at Gloucester: The Most Fascinating House in America.* 1951.
Dogtown Common Trail Map. (Dogtown Advisory Committee.) 1987.
Passport to Greenbelt: A Guide to Open Space in Essex County. (Essex County Greenbelt Association.) 1988.
Pope, Eleanor. *The Wilds of Cape Ann: A Guide to the Natural Areas of Essex, Gloucester, Manchester and Rockport, Massachusetts.* (Resources for Cape Ann.) 1981.
Robbins, Sarah F., & Clarice M. Yentsch. *The Sea is all about us: A guidebook to the marine environments of Cape Ann and other northern New England waters.* 1973.
Shaler, Nathaniel S. *The Geology of Cape Ann, Massachusetts.* 1888.
The Taste of Gloucester: A Fisherman's Wife Cooks. (Fishermen's Wives of Gloucester & Cape Ann League of Women Voters.) 1976.
Webber, John S., Jr. *In and around Cape Ann.* 1896.

Literature and the Arts

Connolly, James B. Novels and stories.
Eliot, T. S. ''The Dry Salvages'' (from *Four Quartets*). 1943.
Kipling, Rudyard. *Captains Courageous.* 1897.
O'Gorman, James F. *This Other Gloucester: Occasional Papers on the Arts of Cape Ann, Massachusetts.* 1976.
Parsons, Peter, & Peter Anastas. *When Gloucester Was Gloucester: Toward an Oral History of the City.* 1973.
Portrait of a Place: Some American Landscape Painters in Gloucester. (Gloucester 350th Anniversary Celebration, Inc.) 1973.
Stockbridge, Clayton B. *Gloucester Story.* (Russel Crouse Prize Play.) 1953.
Walton, Mason A. *A Hermit's Wild Friends: Or Eighteen Years in the Woods.* 1903.
Wilmerding, John. *Fitz Hugh Lane.* 1971.

The poetry of Peter Davison, Clarence M. Falt, Vincent Ferrini, and Charles Olson.

INDEX